Charvona

Ministers of the States

Bigsan and Teresh

Haman's Children

The Royal Palace

The "Shoshanas Ya'akov" Synagogue

The King's Palace Gate

The integrated translation of Megillas Esther is taken from

THE MARGOLIN EDITION OF THE TORAH

CHUMASH WITH HAFTAROS, THE FIVE MEGILLOS,
AND THE COMPLETE SABBATH PRAYERS

translated by Rabbi Binyamin S. Moore

Additional translations by Rabbi Yaakov Yosef Iskowitz and Deena Nataf

copyright © Feldheim Publishers

PURIMSHPIEL

first printed 2003
second, corrected edition 2008

ISBN 1-58330-596-3

Copyright © 2003 by Feldheim Publishers

All rights reserved.
No part of this publication may be translated, reproduced, stored in a retrieval system or transmitted, in any form or by any means, electronic, mechanical, photocopying, recording or otherwise, without prior permission in writing from the publishers.

FELDHEIM PUBLISHERS

POB 43163, Jerusalem, Israel / 208 Airport Executive Park, Nanuet, NY 10954
www.feldheim.com

10 9 8 7 6 5 4 3 2 1

Printed in Israel

"Everything is foreseen, yet free will is granted."
Nevertheless, every event on the "stage of life" occurs
exactly according to the script written by the "Director"
– He Who created the characters, watches over them,
assigns the roles, and controls everything.

PurimShpiel

by Gadi Pollack

The events in the Book of Esther
presented in the light of Midrashic sources,
with the addition of humorous details
and whimsical touches in the spirit
of the traditional "Purim play".

FELDHEIM PUBLISHERS
JERUSALEM   NEW YORK

I thank the Creator of the World Who bestows favor on the undeserving, for the miracles and wonders, and for all the good that He granted me.

GP.

It will take time to figure everything out...

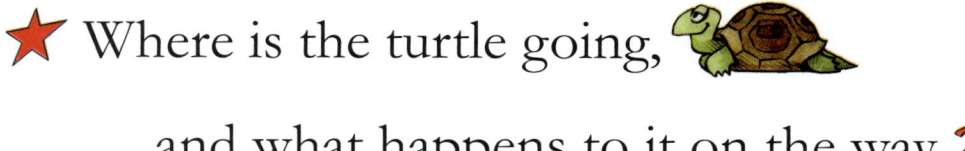

★ Where is the turtle going,

and what happens to it on the way?

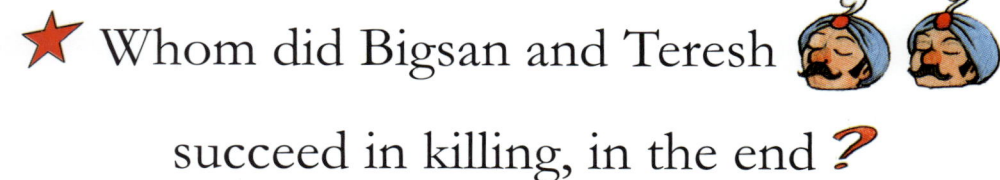

★ Whom did Bigsan and Teresh

succeed in killing, in the end?

★ How did Haman's picture bring about

the pouring of the chamber-pot on his head?

★ And what is the connection

between the concrete ball on the sidewalk

and the nest on the roof?

Look carefully for all the details, all the hints and the hidden meanings in this book – from page to page, from beginning to end, and again from the beginning...!

Once, the king gave them [Mordechai and Haman] money and sent them out at the head of the forces to conquer the country. Haman used up all his money, and had nothing to give his soldiers. Mordechai, however, had half his money left. Haman asked Mordechai to lend him his money. Mordechai answered, "I will lend it to you only if you sell yourself to me as a slave." Haman accepted that, and Mordechai gave him the loan. *Yalkut Shim'oni 5:8.*

They looked for paper on which to write the bill of sale, but found none. Mordechai then wrote the contract on his footgear. This is what it said:

I, Haman, son of Hamedasa, of the family of Agag, whom King Achashverosh sent to battle ... and have sold myself to him [Mordechai] as a slave. If I do not serve him well, or if I deny that I am his slave, or if I refuse to serve him one day a week, all the days of my life, and the same for my children and children's children unto all generations – or if I hold this sale against him, as Esav hated Ya'akov for the sale of his birthright – may a tree of mine be chopped down and may I be hanged on it. So I, Haman, son of Hamedasa, of the family of Agag, fully consent to be the slave of Mordechai the Jew, as it is all written in this contract. *Translation according to Menos ha-Levi.*

> See source material from Midrash and Chazal at the end of the book.

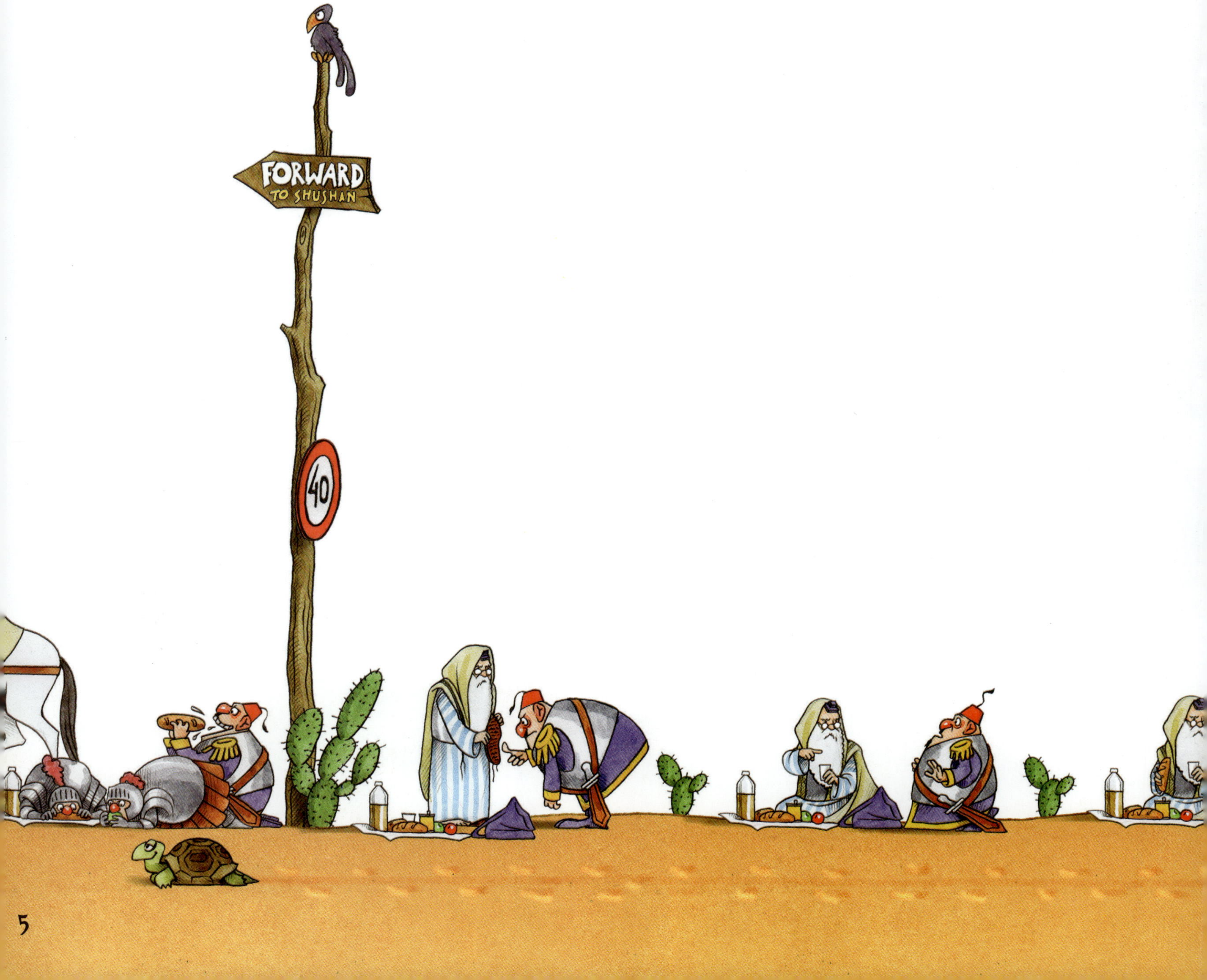

FORWARD
TO SHUSHAN

40

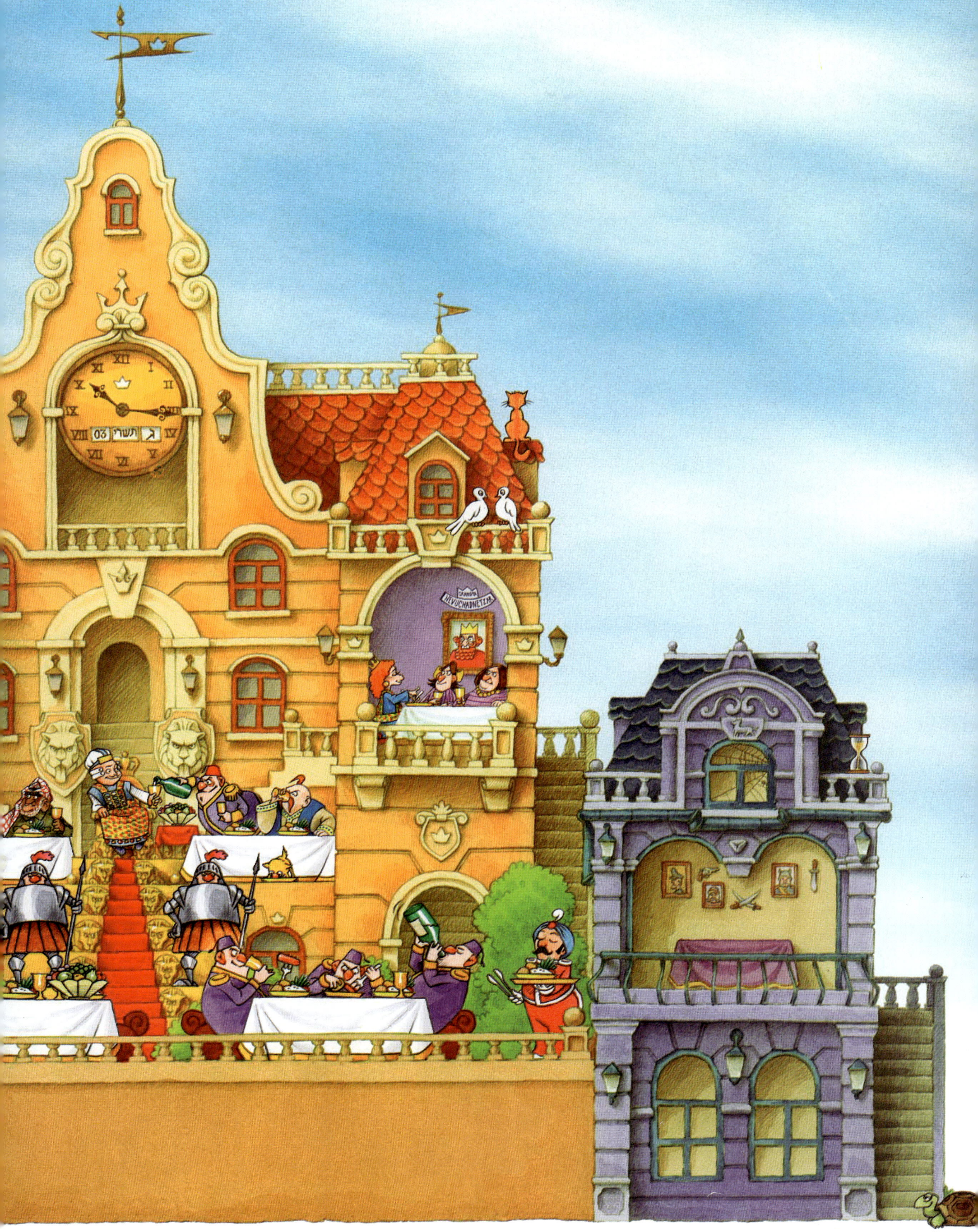

6

א א וַיְהִי בִּימֵי אֲחַשְׁוֵרוֹשׁ הוּא אֲחַשְׁוֵרוֹשׁ הַמֹּלֵךְ מֵהֹדּוּ וְעַד־כּוּשׁ שֶׁבַע וְעֶשְׂרִים וּמֵאָה מְדִינָה: ב בַּיָּמִים הָהֵם כְּשֶׁבֶת הַמֶּלֶךְ אֲחַשְׁוֵרוֹשׁ עַל כִּסֵּא מַלְכוּתוֹ אֲשֶׁר בְּשׁוּשַׁן הַבִּירָה: ג בִּשְׁנַת שָׁלוֹשׁ לְמָלְכוֹ עָשָׂה מִשְׁתֶּה לְכָל־שָׂרָיו וַעֲבָדָיו חֵיל פָּרַס וּמָדַי הַפַּרְתְּמִים וְשָׂרֵי הַמְּדִינוֹת לְפָנָיו: ד בְּהַרְאֹתוֹ אֶת־עֹשֶׁר כְּבוֹד מַלְכוּתוֹ וְאֶת־יְקָר תִּפְאֶרֶת גְּדוּלָּתוֹ יָמִים רַבִּים שְׁמוֹנִים וּמְאַת יוֹם: ה וּבִמְלוֹאת ק׳ וּבִמְלֹאת הַיָּמִים הָאֵלֶּה עָשָׂה הַמֶּלֶךְ לְכָל־הָעָם הַנִּמְצְאִים בְּשׁוּשַׁן הַבִּירָה לְמִגָּדוֹל וְעַד־קָטָן מִשְׁתֶּה שִׁבְעַת יָמִים בַּחֲצַר גִּנַּת בִּיתַן הַמֶּלֶךְ: ו חוּר ח׳ יְתֵרָה כַּרְפַּס וּתְכֵלֶת אָחוּז בְּחַבְלֵי־בוּץ וְאַרְגָּמָן עַל גְּלִילֵי כֶסֶף וְעַמּוּדֵי שֵׁשׁ מִטּוֹת זָהָב וָכֶסֶף עַל רִצְפַת בַּהַט־וָשֵׁשׁ וְדַר וְסֹחָרֶת: ז וְהַשְׁקוֹת בִּכְלֵי זָהָב וְכֵלִים מִכֵּלִים שׁוֹנִים וְיֵין מַלְכוּת רָב כְּיַד הַמֶּלֶךְ: ח וְהַשְּׁתִיָּה כַדָּת אֵין אֹנֵס כִּי־כֵן יִסַּד הַמֶּלֶךְ עַל כָּל־רַב בֵּיתוֹ לַעֲשׂוֹת כִּרְצוֹן אִישׁ־וָאִישׁ: ט גַּם וַשְׁתִּי הַמַּלְכָּה עָשְׂתָה מִשְׁתֵּה נָשִׁים בֵּית הַמַּלְכוּת אֲשֶׁר לַמֶּלֶךְ אֲחַשְׁוֵרוֹשׁ:

1 [1] IT HAPPENED IN THE DAYS OF ACHASHVEROSH—he is [the same] Achashverosh who was ruling over a hundred and twenty-seven states [in the same way as he ruled] from Hodu to Kush: [2] At that time, when King Achashverosh had consolidated his rule over his kingdom, whose seat was in Shushan the capital—[3] in the third year of his reign—he made a banquet for all his ministers and servants, [with] the army of Paras and Madai [and] the governors and ministers of the states [all being present]. [4] [This was] when he displayed the wealth of his royal glory and the magnificence of the majesty of his greatness. [The banquet lasted] for many days—one hundred and eighty days. [5] And when these days ended, the king made a seven-day banquet for all the people located in Shushan, the capital, from the greatest to the most insignificant, in the courtyard, garden [and] orchard of the king. [6] White, parsley-green and aquamarine [sheets], embroidered with fine linen and purple [wool] cords, [were spread] over silver wheels and marble pillars, [and] golden and silver couches [were set up] on a flooring of bahat, marble, dar and sochares [stone]. [7] And [the king ordered that the guests] be given to drink in golden vessels and [other] various kinds of vessels, and [there was] much royal wine, as [befitted] the king's wealth. [8] And [any amount of] drink was in order [since] there was no compulsion, for so the king had decreed upon every official of his household to carry out the [individual] wishes of each person. [9] Queen Vashti also made a women's banquet at King Achashverosh's royal palace.

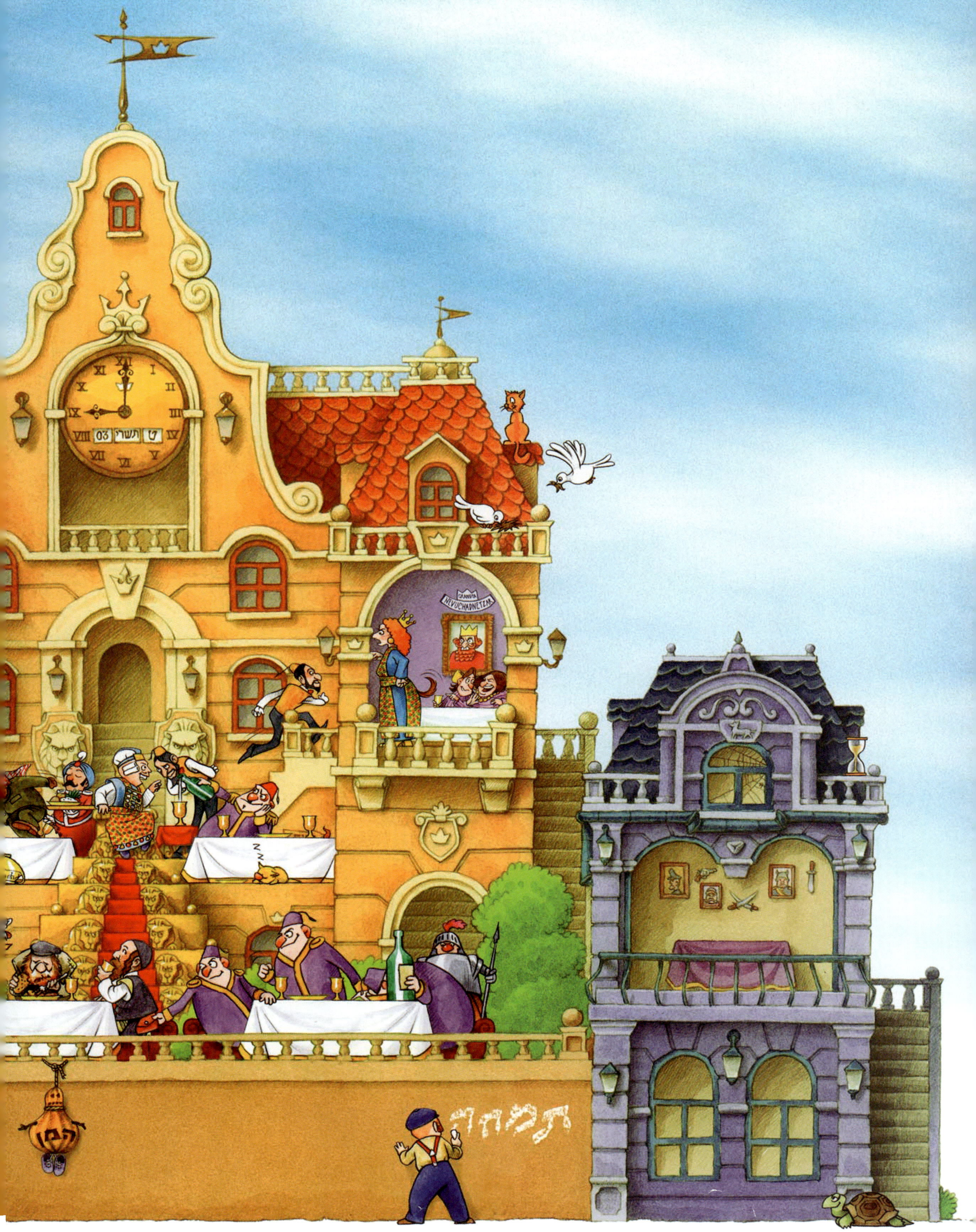

תפוחה

י בַּיּוֹם הַשְּׁבִיעִי כְּטוֹב לֵב הַמֶּלֶךְ בַּיָּיִן אָמַר לִמְהוּמָן בִּזְּתָא חַרְבוֹנָא בִּגְתָא וַאֲבַגְתָא זֵתַר וְכַרְכַּס שִׁבְעַת הַסָּרִיסִים הַמְשָׁרְתִים אֶת פְּנֵי הַמֶּלֶךְ אֲחַשְׁוֵרוֹשׁ: יא לְהָבִיא אֶת וַשְׁתִּי הַמַּלְכָּה לִפְנֵי הַמֶּלֶךְ בְּכֶתֶר מַלְכוּת לְהַרְאוֹת הָעַמִּים וְהַשָּׂרִים אֶת יָפְיָהּ כִּי טוֹבַת מַרְאֶה הִיא:

[10] On the seventh day, when the king was merry with wine, he told Mehuman, Bizesa, Charvona, Bigsa, Avagsa, Zesar and Karkas, the seven attendants who waited upon King Achashverosh, [11] to bring Queen Vashti before the king [wearing her] royal crown, to show the nations and the nobles her beauty, for she was [indeed] of fine appearance.

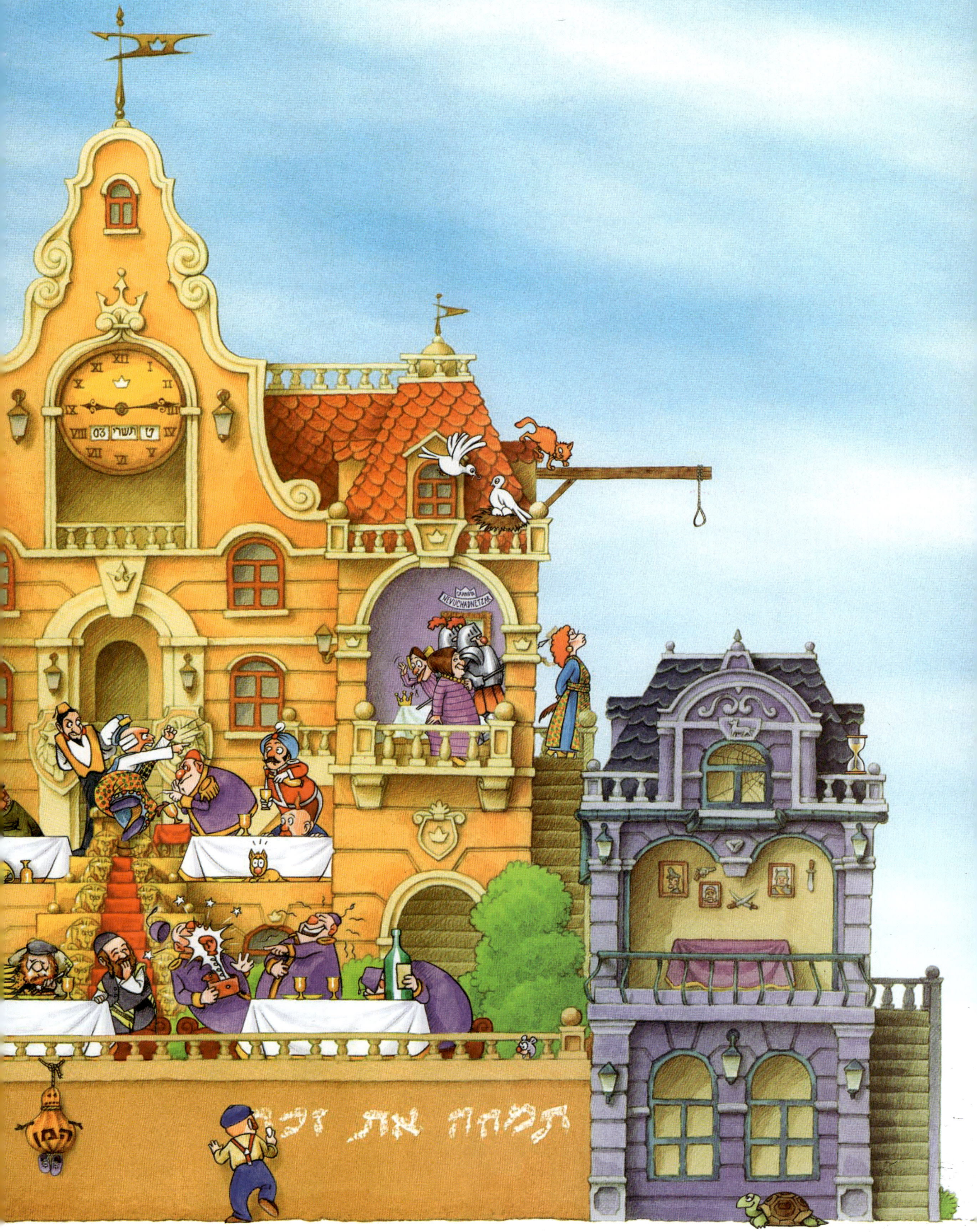

תמצא את ז'ו

יב וַתְּמָאֵן הַמַּלְכָּה וַשְׁתִּי לָבוֹא בִּדְבַר הַמֶּלֶךְ אֲשֶׁר בְּיַד הַסָּרִיסִים וַיִּקְצֹף הַמֶּלֶךְ מְאֹד וַחֲמָתוֹ בָּעֲרָה בוֹ: יג וַיֹּאמֶר הַמֶּלֶךְ לַחֲכָמִים יֹדְעֵי הָעִתִּים כִּי כֵן דְּבַר הַמֶּלֶךְ לִפְנֵי כָּל יֹדְעֵי דָּת וָדִין: יד וְהַקָּרֹב אֵלָיו כַּרְשְׁנָא שֵׁתָר אַדְמָתָא תַרְשִׁישׁ מֶרֶס מַרְסְנָא מְמוּכָן שִׁבְעַת שָׂרֵי פָּרַס וּמָדַי רֹאֵי פְּנֵי הַמֶּלֶךְ הַיֹּשְׁבִים רִאשֹׁנָה בַּמַּלְכוּת: טו כְּדָת מַה לַּעֲשׂוֹת בַּמַּלְכָּה וַשְׁתִּי עַל אֲשֶׁר לֹא עָשְׂתָה אֶת מַאֲמַר הַמֶּלֶךְ אֲחַשְׁוֵרוֹשׁ בְּיַד הַסָּרִיסִים: טז וַיֹּאמֶר מומכן מְמוּכָן לִפְנֵי הַמֶּלֶךְ וְהַשָּׂרִים לֹא עַל הַמֶּלֶךְ לְבַדּוֹ עָוְתָה וַשְׁתִּי הַמַּלְכָּה כִּי עַל כָּל הַשָּׂרִים וְעַל כָּל הָעַמִּים אֲשֶׁר בְּכָל מְדִינוֹת הַמֶּלֶךְ אֲחַשְׁוֵרוֹשׁ: יז כִּי יֵצֵא דְבַר הַמַּלְכָּה עַל כָּל הַנָּשִׁים לְהַבְזוֹת בַּעְלֵיהֶן בְּעֵינֵיהֶן בְּאָמְרָם הַמֶּלֶךְ אֲחַשְׁוֵרוֹשׁ אָמַר לְהָבִיא אֶת וַשְׁתִּי הַמַּלְכָּה לְפָנָיו וְלֹא בָאָה: יח וְהַיּוֹם הַזֶּה תֹּאמַרְנָה שָׂרוֹת פָּרַס וּמָדַי אֲשֶׁר שָׁמְעוּ אֶת דְּבַר הַמַּלְכָּה לְכֹל שָׂרֵי הַמֶּלֶךְ וּכְדַי בִּזָּיוֹן וָקָצֶף: יט אִם עַל הַמֶּלֶךְ טוֹב יֵצֵא דְבַר מַלְכוּת מִלְּפָנָיו וְיִכָּתֵב בְּדָתֵי פָרַס וּמָדַי וְלֹא יַעֲבוֹר אֲשֶׁר לֹא תָבוֹא וַשְׁתִּי לִפְנֵי הַמֶּלֶךְ אֲחַשְׁוֵרוֹשׁ וּמַלְכוּתָהּ יִתֵּן הַמֶּלֶךְ לִרְעוּתָהּ הַטּוֹבָה מִמֶּנָּה: כ וְנִשְׁמַע פִּתְגָם הַמֶּלֶךְ אֲשֶׁר יַעֲשֶׂה בְּכָל מַלְכוּתוֹ כִּי רַבָּה הִיא וְכָל הַנָּשִׁים יִתְּנוּ יְקָר לְבַעְלֵיהֶן לְמִגָּדוֹל וְעַד קָטָן: כא וַיִּיטַב הַדָּבָר בְּעֵינֵי הַמֶּלֶךְ וְהַשָּׂרִים וַיַּעַשׂ הַמֶּלֶךְ כִּדְבַר מְמוּכָן: כב וַיִּשְׁלַח סְפָרִים אֶל כָּל מְדִינוֹת הַמֶּלֶךְ אֶל מְדִינָה וּמְדִינָה כִּכְתָבָהּ וְאֶל עַם וָעָם כִּלְשׁוֹנוֹ לִהְיוֹת כָּל אִישׁ שֹׂרֵר בְּבֵיתוֹ וּמְדַבֵּר כִּלְשׁוֹן עַמּוֹ:

[12] But Queen Vashti refused to come at the order of the king that [he had sent] through [his] attendants, and [so] the king was extremely enraged and his fury burned within him. [13] The king then consulted the wise men, experts in astronomy, for so was the king's [practice to present every] matter before all the law and judicial experts. [14] And his close [advisers] were Karshena, Shesar, Admasa, Tarshish, Meres, Marsena and Memuchan, the seven ministers of Paras and Madai who had [constant] access to the king [and] were the highest members of the realm. [15] [He consulted them as to] what, according to law, should be done with Queen Vashti, for that she did not carry out the decree of King Achashverosh [which he had sent] with his attendants. [16] Memuchan then said before the king and the ministers, "Not only against the king did Queen Vashti act disobediently, but [also] against all the ministers and all the nations who [live] in all the states of King Achashverosh. [17] For the incident of the queen will spread among all the women [and cause them] to belittle their husbands, when [the nobles] tell [that] King Achashverosh ordered to have Queen Vashti brought before him but she did not come. [18] And [even] today, the ladies of Paras and Madai who heard about the incident of the queen will tell all the ministers of the king [about it], and this [will cause] much humiliation and anger. [19] If it pleases the king, let a royal proclamation be issued by him, and let it be inscribed among the laws of Paras and Madai and not be revoked, that Vashti would not come before King Achashverosh [and was therefore killed], and so the king will grant her royal [position] to her counterpart who is better than her. [20] The king's decree that he will enact shall then be publicized throughout his kingdom, for it is a great [decree], and [thus] all women will give respect to their husbands, whether great or insignificant." [21] The matter pleased the king and the ministers, and the king carried out what Memuchan had said. [22] He sent bills [of law] to all the king's states, to each state according to its [form of] script, and to each nation according to its language, [stating] that every man be the ruler in his house, and that [his wife] speak his language.

שמחת יום עמלה

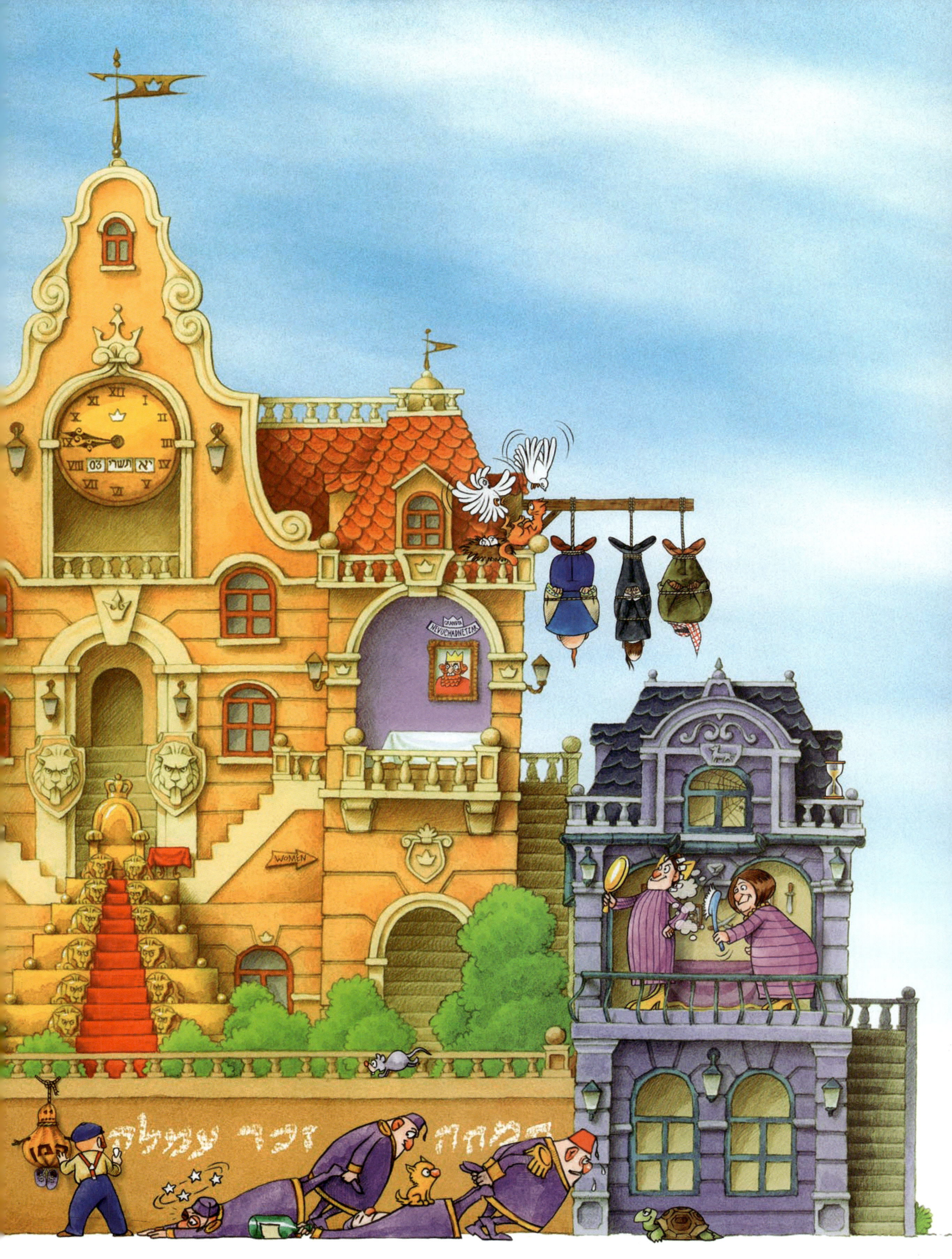

ב א אַחַר הַדְּבָרִים הָאֵלֶּה כְּשֹׁךְ חֲמַת הַמֶּלֶךְ אֲחַשְׁוֵרוֹשׁ זָכַר אֶת וַשְׁתִּי וְאֵת אֲשֶׁר עָשָׂתָה וְאֵת אֲשֶׁר נִגְזַר עָלֶיהָ: ב וַיֹּאמְרוּ נַעֲרֵי הַמֶּלֶךְ מְשָׁרְתָיו יְבַקְשׁוּ לַמֶּלֶךְ נְעָרוֹת בְּתוּלוֹת טוֹבוֹת מַרְאֶה: ג וְיַפְקֵד הַמֶּלֶךְ פְּקִידִים בְּכָל מְדִינוֹת מַלְכוּתוֹ וְיִקְבְּצוּ אֶת כָּל נַעֲרָה בְתוּלָה טוֹבַת מַרְאֶה אֶל שׁוּשַׁן הַבִּירָה אֶל בֵּית הַנָּשִׁים אֶל יַד הֵגֶא סְרִיס הַמֶּלֶךְ שֹׁמֵר הַנָּשִׁים וְנָתוֹן תַּמְרוּקֵיהֶן: ד וְהַנַּעֲרָה אֲשֶׁר תִּיטַב בְּעֵינֵי הַמֶּלֶךְ תִּמְלֹךְ תַּחַת וַשְׁתִּי וַיִּיטַב הַדָּבָר בְּעֵינֵי הַמֶּלֶךְ וַיַּעַשׂ כֵּן:

2 [1] AFTER THESE EVENTS, when King Achashverosh's anger had abated, he remembered Vashti and what she had done, and what had been decreed upon her. [2] So the king's young men, his servants, said to him, "Let [the king's messengers] look for good-looking young maidens for the king. [3] Let the king appoint officers in all the states of his kingdom, and they shall bring together every good-looking young maiden to Shushan the capital, to the women's residence, into the charge of Hegey, the king's attendant, the guardian of the women, with their cosmetics being provided. [4] Then, the young girl who is pleasing in the eyes of the king shall become queen instead of Vashti." The idea pleased the king and he did so.

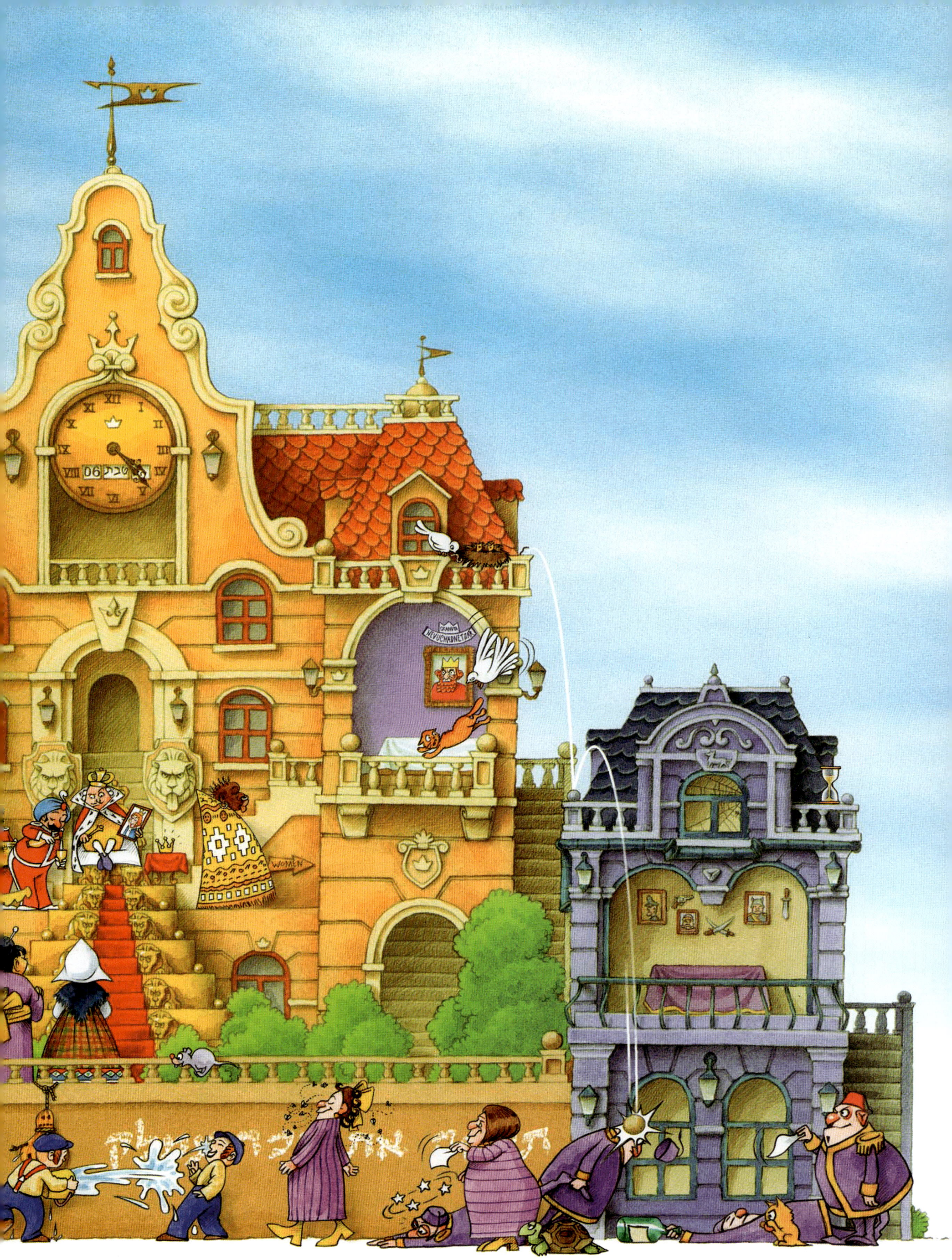

14

ח אִישׁ יְהוּדִי הָיָה בְּשׁוּשַׁן הַבִּירָה וּשְׁמוֹ מָרְדֳּכַי בֶּן יָאִיר בֶּן שִׁמְעִי בֶּן קִישׁ אִישׁ יְמִינִי: י אֲשֶׁר הָגְלָה מִירוּשָׁלַיִם עִם הַגֹּלָה אֲשֶׁר הָגְלְתָה עִם יְכָנְיָה מֶלֶךְ יְהוּדָה אֲשֶׁר הֶגְלָה נְבוּכַדְנֶאצַּר מֶלֶךְ בָּבֶל: ז וַיְהִי אֹמֵן אֶת הֲדַסָּה הִיא אֶסְתֵּר בַּת דֹּדוֹ כִּי אֵין לָהּ אָב וָאֵם וְהַנַּעֲרָה יְפַת תֹּאַר וְטוֹבַת מַרְאֶה וּבְמוֹת אָבִיהָ וְאִמָּהּ לְקָחָהּ מָרְדֳּכַי לוֹ לְבַת: ח וַיְהִי בְּהִשָּׁמַע דְּבַר הַמֶּלֶךְ וְדָתוֹ וּבְהִקָּבֵץ נְעָרוֹת רַבּוֹת אֶל שׁוּשַׁן הַבִּירָה אֶל יַד הֵגָי וַתִּלָּקַח אֶסְתֵּר אֶל בֵּית הַמֶּלֶךְ אֶל יַד הֵגַי שֹׁמֵר הַנָּשִׁים: ט וַתִּיטַב הַנַּעֲרָה בְעֵינָיו וַתִּשָּׂא חֶסֶד לְפָנָיו וַיְבַהֵל אֶת תַּמְרוּקֶיהָ וְאֶת מָנוֹתֶהָ לָתֵת לָהּ וְאֵת שֶׁבַע הַנְּעָרוֹת הָרְאֻיוֹת לָתֶת לָהּ מִבֵּית הַמֶּלֶךְ וַיְשַׁנֶּהָ וְאֶת נַעֲרוֹתֶיהָ לְטוֹב בֵּית הַנָּשִׁים: י לֹא הִגִּידָה אֶסְתֵּר אֶת עַמָּהּ וְאֶת מוֹלַדְתָּהּ כִּי מָרְדֳּכַי צִוָּה עָלֶיהָ אֲשֶׁר לֹא תַגִּיד: יא וּבְכָל יוֹם וָיוֹם מָרְדֳּכַי מִתְהַלֵּךְ לִפְנֵי חֲצַר בֵּית הַנָּשִׁים לָדַעַת אֶת שְׁלוֹם אֶסְתֵּר וּמַה יֵּעָשֶׂה בָּהּ: יב וּבְהַגִּיעַ תֹּר נַעֲרָה וְנַעֲרָה לָבוֹא אֶל הַמֶּלֶךְ אֲחַשְׁוֵרוֹשׁ מִקֵּץ הֱיוֹת לָהּ כְּדָת הַנָּשִׁים שְׁנֵים עָשָׂר חֹדֶשׁ כִּי כֵּן יִמְלְאוּ יְמֵי מְרוּקֵיהֶן שִׁשָּׁה חֳדָשִׁים בְּשֶׁמֶן הַמֹּר וְשִׁשָּׁה חֳדָשִׁים בַּבְּשָׂמִים וּבְתַמְרוּקֵי הַנָּשִׁים: יג וּבָזֶה הַנַּעֲרָה בָּאָה אֶל הַמֶּלֶךְ אֵת כָּל אֲשֶׁר תֹּאמַר יִנָּתֵן לָהּ לָבוֹא עִמָּהּ מִבֵּית הַנָּשִׁים עַד בֵּית הַמֶּלֶךְ: יד בָּעֶרֶב הִיא בָאָה וּבַבֹּקֶר הִיא שָׁבָה אֶל בֵּית הַנָּשִׁים שֵׁנִי אֶל יַד שַׁעֲשְׁגַז סְרִיס הַמֶּלֶךְ שֹׁמֵר הַפִּילַגְשִׁים לֹא תָבוֹא עוֹד אֶל הַמֶּלֶךְ כִּי אִם חָפֵץ בָּהּ הַמֶּלֶךְ וְנִקְרְאָה בְשֵׁם:

[5] **There was a Jewish man in Shushan the capital, whose name was Mordechai, the son of Ya'ir, the son of Shim'iy, the son of Kish, a man of [the tribe of] Binyamin;** [6] who had been exiled from Yerushalayim, with the exile that was exiled with Yechonyah, the king of Yehudah, whom Nevuchadnetzar, the king of Bavel, had exiled. [7] He took care of Hadassah—that is Esther, his cousin—for she had no father or mother. Now, the girl was beautifully formed and of fine appearance, and when her father and mother died, Mordechai took her for himself as a [wife]. [8] It was then, when the king's proclamation and law were publicized, and many girls were brought together to Shushan the capital, into the charge of Hegai, that Esther was [also] taken to the king's palace, into the charge of Hegai, the guardian of the women. [9] The girl was pleasing to him and carried favor with him, so he hurriedly brought her her cosmetics and her portions [of food], and the seven maids she was allocated from the king's palace [to serve her], and he gave her and her maids preferential treatment [at] the women's residence. [10] Esther did not tell [them] her nationality or lineage, because Mordechai had ordered her that she must not tell. [11] And each day Mordechai would walk in front of the courtyard of the women's residence, to find out how Esther was faring and what was happening to her. [12] And when the time came for each girl to go to King Achashverosh—at the end of her having had the prescribed [time] for women, twelve months, for that is the duration of their cosmetic process: six months with myrrh oil and six months with perfumes and women's cosmetics—[13] in this [way] the girl would go to the king: whatever she asked would be given to her, to accompany her from the women's residence to the king's palace. [14] In the evening she would go [to the king], and in the morning she would return to the second women's residence, into the charge of Sha'ashgaz, the king's attendant, the guardian of the concubines. She would not go again to the king, unless the king desired her and she was called by name.

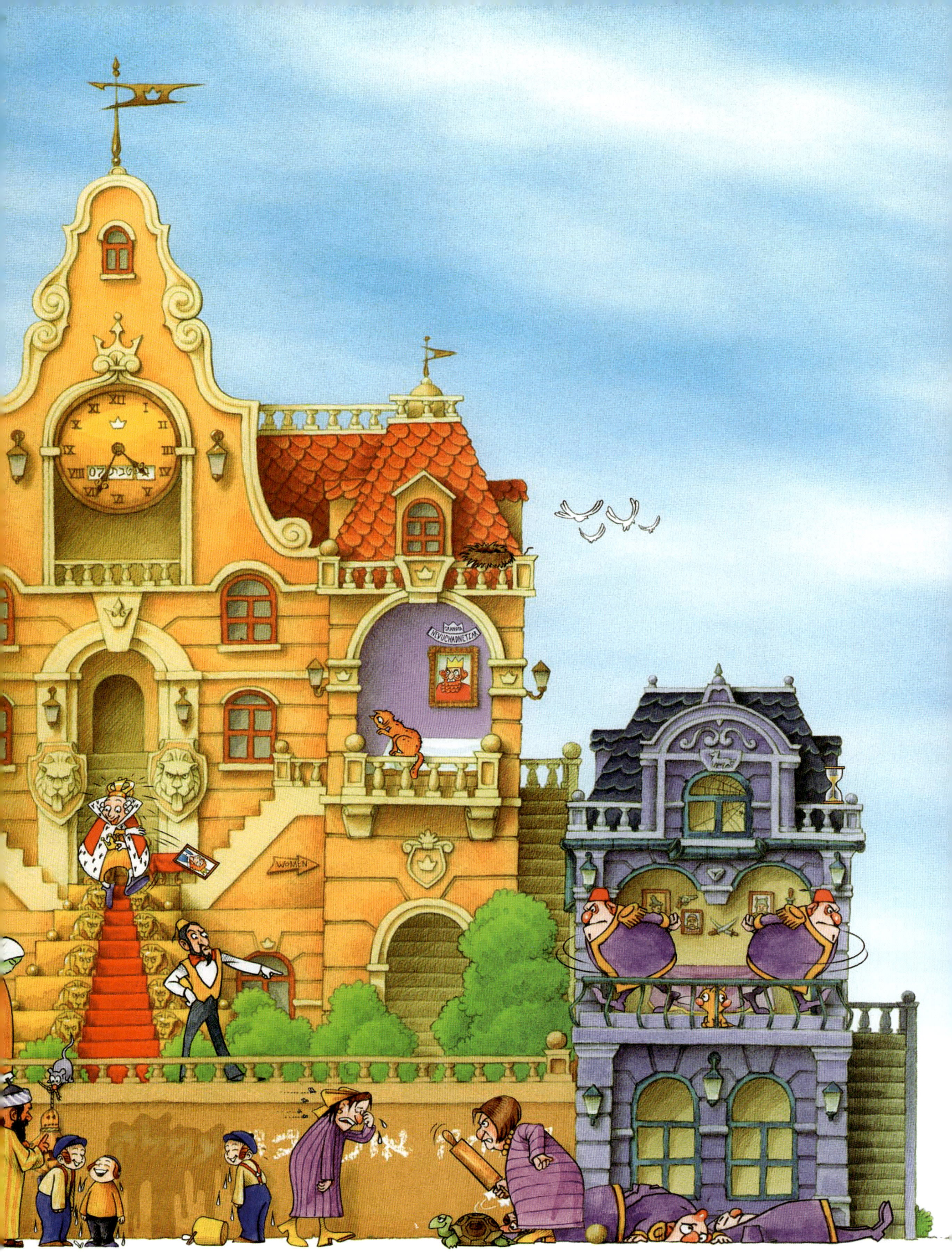

16

טו וּבְהַגִּיעַ תֹּר־אֶסְתֵּר בַּת־אֲבִיחַיִל דֹּד מָרְדֳּכַי אֲשֶׁר לָקַח־לוֹ לְבַת לָבוֹא אֶל־הַמֶּלֶךְ לֹא בִקְשָׁה דָּבָר כִּי אִם אֶת־אֲשֶׁר יֹאמַר הֵגַי סְרִיס־הַמֶּלֶךְ שֹׁמֵר הַנָּשִׁים וַתְּהִי אֶסְתֵּר נֹשֵׂאת חֵן בְּעֵינֵי כָּל־רֹאֶיהָ: טז וַתִּלָּקַח אֶסְתֵּר אֶל־הַמֶּלֶךְ אֲחַשְׁוֵרוֹשׁ אֶל־בֵּית מַלְכוּתוֹ בַּחֹדֶשׁ הָעֲשִׂירִי הוּא־חֹדֶשׁ טֵבֵת בִּשְׁנַת־שֶׁבַע לְמַלְכוּתוֹ: יז וַיֶּאֱהַב הַמֶּלֶךְ אֶת־אֶסְתֵּר מִכָּל־הַנָּשִׁים וַתִּשָּׂא־חֵן וָחֶסֶד לְפָנָיו מִכָּל־הַבְּתוּלֹת וַיָּשֶׂם כֶּתֶר־מַלְכוּת בְּרֹאשָׁהּ וַיַּמְלִיכֶהָ תַּחַת וַשְׁתִּי: יח וַיַּעַשׂ הַמֶּלֶךְ מִשְׁתֶּה גָדוֹל לְכָל־שָׂרָיו וַעֲבָדָיו אֵת מִשְׁתֵּה אֶסְתֵּר וַהֲנָחָה לַמְּדִינוֹת עָשָׂה וַיִּתֵּן מַשְׂאֵת כְּיַד הַמֶּלֶךְ: יט וּבְהִקָּבֵץ בְּתוּלוֹת שֵׁנִית וּמָרְדֳּכַי יֹשֵׁב בְּשַׁעַר־הַמֶּלֶךְ: כ אֵין אֶסְתֵּר מַגֶּדֶת מוֹלַדְתָּהּ וְאֶת־עַמָּהּ כַּאֲשֶׁר צִוָּה עָלֶיהָ מָרְדֳּכָי וְאֶת־מַאֲמַר מָרְדֳּכַי אֶסְתֵּר עֹשָׂה כַּאֲשֶׁר הָיְתָה בְאָמְנָה אִתּוֹ:

[15] And when the time came for Esther—the daughter of Avichayil, the uncle of Mordechai who had taken [her] for himself as a [wife]—to go to the king, she did not request anything, except for what Hegai, the king's attendant, the guardian of the women, would say [be given to her]. [Nevertheless,] Esther carried charm before everyone who saw her. [16] Esther was taken to King Achashverosh, to his royal palace, in the tenth month, which is the month of Teves, in the seventh year of his reign. [17] The king loved Esther more than all the [other] women, and she carried charm and favor before him more than all the [other] maidens, so he placed the royal crown on her head, and made her queen in place of Vashti. [18] The king then made a great banquet for all his ministers and servants, [calling it] Esther's banquet, and made a [tax] concession for the states and gave [them] king-size gifts. [19] And when the maidens were brought together a second time, [nevertheless, since] Mordechai was sitting at the king's [palace] gate, [20] Esther would not tell [the king] her lineage or nationality, just as Mordechai had ordered her. Esther [also] carried out all [the laws] that Mordechai had told her [to do], just as when she was in his care.

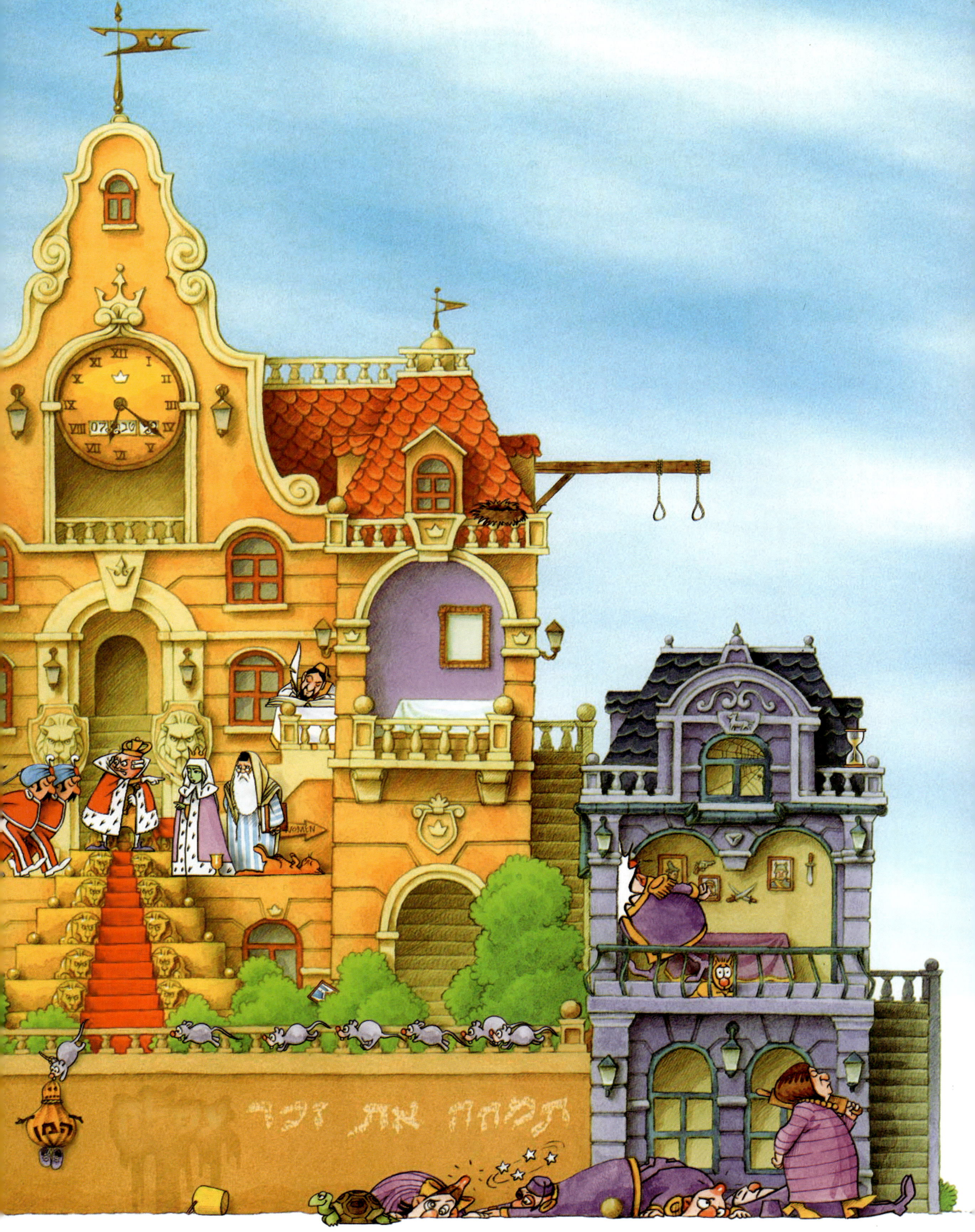

הפכת את דני

²¹ At that time, when Mordechai was sitting at the king's [palace] gate, Bigsan and Teresh, two attendants of the king, of the guards of the inner court, were angry, and conspired to act against King Achashverosh. ²² Mordechai found out about the [conspiracy] and told Queen Esther [about it]. Esther then informed the king, in the name of Mordechai. ²³ The matter was then investigated and found [to be true], and both [Bigsan and Teresh] were hanged on a gallows. [Mordechai's deed] was written down in the book of chronicles [that was kept] before the king.

כא בַּיָּמִים הָהֵם וּמָרְדֳּכַי יוֹשֵׁב בְּשַׁעַר הַמֶּלֶךְ קָצַף בִּגְתָן וָתֶרֶשׁ שְׁנֵי סָרִיסֵי הַמֶּלֶךְ מִשֹּׁמְרֵי הַסַּף וַיְבַקְשׁוּ לִשְׁלֹחַ יָד בַּמֶּלֶךְ אֲחַשְׁוֵרֹשׁ: כב וַיִּוָּדַע הַדָּבָר לְמָרְדֳּכַי וַיַּגֵּד לְאֶסְתֵּר הַמַּלְכָּה וַתֹּאמֶר אֶסְתֵּר לַמֶּלֶךְ בְּשֵׁם מָרְדֳּכָי: כג וַיְבֻקַּשׁ הַדָּבָר וַיִּמָּצֵא וַיִּתָּלוּ שְׁנֵיהֶם עַל עֵץ וַיִּכָּתֵב בְּסֵפֶר דִּבְרֵי הַיָּמִים לִפְנֵי הַמֶּלֶךְ:

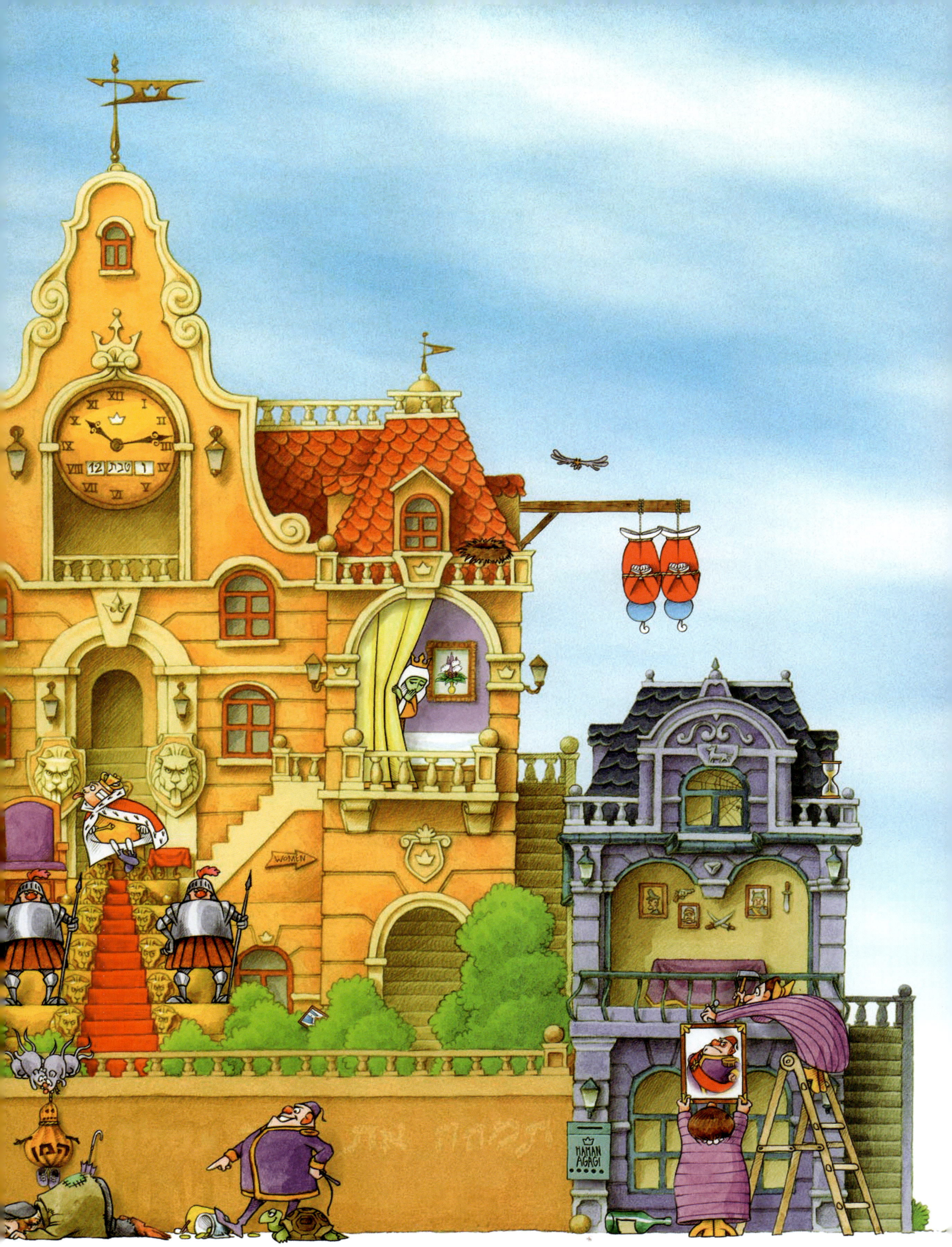
ו טבת 12
WOMEN
HAMAN AGAGI

ג א אַחַר הַדְּבָרִים הָאֵלֶּה גִּדַּל הַמֶּלֶךְ אֲחַשְׁוֵרוֹשׁ אֶת־הָמָן בֶּן־הַמְּדָתָא הָאֲגָגִי וַיְנַשְּׂאֵהוּ וַיָּשֶׂם אֶת־כִּסְאוֹ מֵעַל כָּל־הַשָּׂרִים אֲשֶׁר אִתּוֹ: ב וְכָל־עַבְדֵי הַמֶּלֶךְ אֲשֶׁר־בְּשַׁעַר הַמֶּלֶךְ כֹּרְעִים וּמִשְׁתַּחֲוִים לְהָמָן כִּי־כֵן צִוָּה־לוֹ הַמֶּלֶךְ וּמָרְדֳּכַי לֹא יִכְרַע וְלֹא יִשְׁתַּחֲוֶה: ג וַיֹּאמְרוּ עַבְדֵי הַמֶּלֶךְ אֲשֶׁר־בְּשַׁעַר הַמֶּלֶךְ לְמָרְדֳּכָי מַדּוּעַ אַתָּה עוֹבֵר אֵת מִצְוַת הַמֶּלֶךְ: ד וַיְהִי בְּאָמְרָם כּאָמְרָם ק׳ אֵלָיו יוֹם וָיוֹם וְלֹא שָׁמַע אֲלֵיהֶם וַיַּגִּידוּ לְהָמָן לִרְאוֹת הֲיַעַמְדוּ דִּבְרֵי מָרְדֳּכַי כִּי־הִגִּיד לָהֶם אֲשֶׁר־הוּא יְהוּדִי: ה וַיַּרְא הָמָן כִּי־אֵין מָרְדֳּכַי כֹּרֵעַ וּמִשְׁתַּחֲוֶה לוֹ וַיִּמָּלֵא הָמָן חֵמָה: ו וַיִּבֶז בְּעֵינָיו לִשְׁלֹחַ יָד בְּמָרְדֳּכַי לְבַדּוֹ כִּי־הִגִּידוּ לוֹ אֶת־עַם מָרְדֳּכָי וַיְבַקֵּשׁ הָמָן לְהַשְׁמִיד אֶת־כָּל־הַיְּהוּדִים אֲשֶׁר בְּכָל־מַלְכוּת אֲחַשְׁוֵרוֹשׁ עַם מָרְדֳּכָי:

3 ¹AFTER THESE EVENTS, King Achashverosh promoted Haman the son of Hamedasa, the Agagi, and raised his status, and made his position higher than all the [other] ministers who were with him. ²And all the king's servants who were at the king's [palace] gate were bowing down and prostrating themselves to Haman, for so the king had commanded regarding him, but Mordechai would not bow down or prostrate himself. ³The king's servants who were at the king's [palace] gate then said to Mordechai, "Why do you disobey the king's command?" ⁴ When they said [this] to him day after day but he did not listen to them, they told Haman [about it], to see if Mordechai's words would hold firm, for he had told them that [he did not bow down because] he was a Jew. ⁵Haman then saw that Mordechai was not bowing down or prostrating himself to him and Haman was filled with rage. ⁶He regarded it below his dignity, [though,] to act against Mordechai alone, [and] since they had told him to which people Mordechai belonged, Haman wished to destroy all the Jews who were in the entire kingdom of Achashverosh—Mordechai's people.

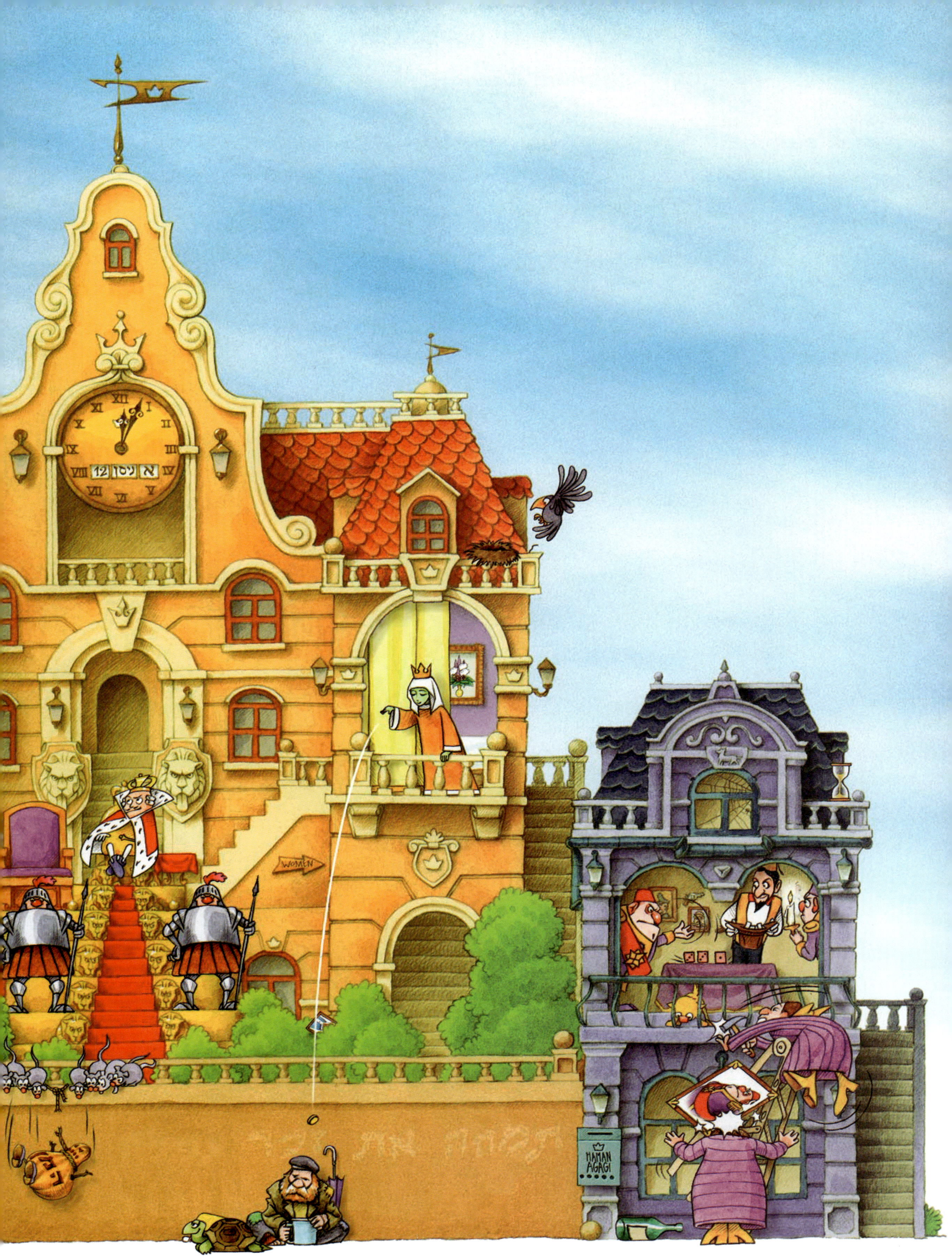
א ניסן 12
WOMEN
HAMAN AGAGI

ז בַּחֹדֶשׁ הָרִאשׁוֹן הוּא חֹדֶשׁ נִיסָן בִּשְׁנַת שְׁתֵּים עֶשְׂרֵה לַמֶּלֶךְ אֲחַשְׁוֵרוֹשׁ הִפִּיל פּוּר הוּא הַגּוֹרָל לִפְנֵי הָמָן מִיּוֹם לְיוֹם וּמֵחֹדֶשׁ לְחֹדֶשׁ שְׁנֵים־עָשָׂר הוּא־חֹדֶשׁ אֲדָר:

[7] In the first month, the month of Nisan, in the twelfth year of King Achashverosh, [someone] cast Pur, which is the lot, before Haman, [to select] which day and which month, [and it came out] to the twelfth month, the month of Adar.

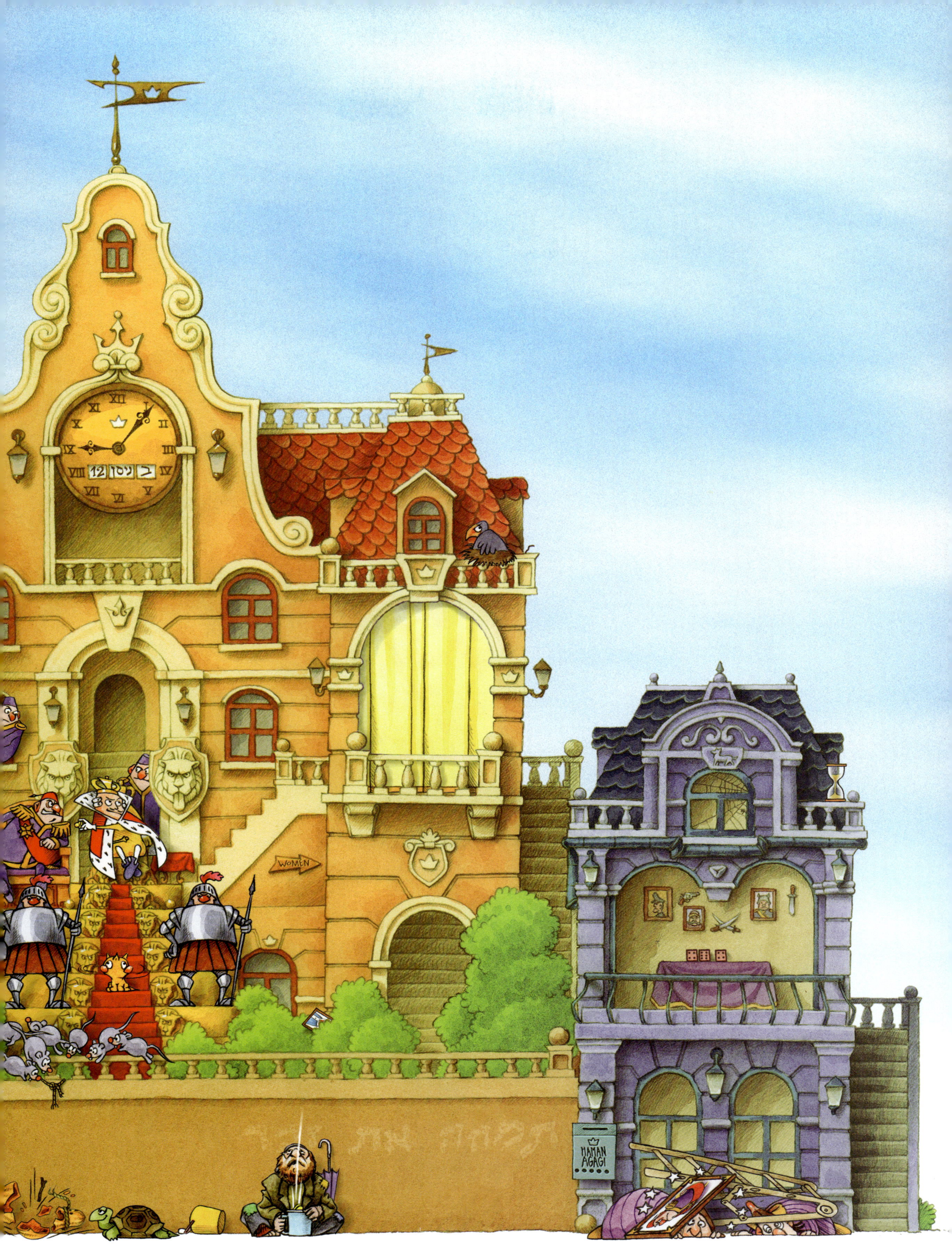

24

ח וַיֹּאמֶר הָמָן לַמֶּלֶךְ אֲחַשְׁוֵרוֹשׁ יֶשְׁנוֹ עַם אֶחָד מְפֻזָּר וּמְפֹרָד בֵּין הָעַמִּים בְּכֹל מְדִינוֹת מַלְכוּתֶךָ וְדָתֵיהֶם שֹׁנוֹת מִכָּל עָם וְאֶת דָּתֵי הַמֶּלֶךְ אֵינָם עֹשִׂים וְלַמֶּלֶךְ אֵין שֹׁוֶה לְהַנִּיחָם: ט אִם עַל הַמֶּלֶךְ טוֹב יִכָּתֵב לְאַבְּדָם וַעֲשֶׂרֶת אֲלָפִים כִּכַּר כֶּסֶף אֶשְׁקוֹל עַל יְדֵי עֹשֵׂי הַמְּלָאכָה לְהָבִיא אֶל גִּנְזֵי הַמֶּלֶךְ: י וַיָּסַר הַמֶּלֶךְ אֶת טַבַּעְתּוֹ מֵעַל יָדוֹ וַיִּתְּנָהּ לְהָמָן בֶּן הַמְּדָתָא הָאֲגָגִי צֹרֵר הַיְּהוּדִים: יא וַיֹּאמֶר הַמֶּלֶךְ לְהָמָן הַכֶּסֶף נָתוּן לָךְ וְהָעָם לַעֲשׂוֹת בּוֹ כַּטּוֹב בְּעֵינֶיךָ:

[8] Haman then said to King Achashverosh, "There is a certain people, scattered and spread out among the [other] peoples in all the states of your kingdom, and their laws are different from [those of] other peoples and they do not observe the king's laws, so it is not worth it for the king to leave them alive. [9] If it pleases the king, let [a decree] be written to annihilate them, and I shall have ten thousand kikar of silver weighed out by the mint to be brought to the king's treasuries." [10] The king then removed his signet ring from his hand and gave it to Haman the son of Hamedasa, the Agagi, the oppressor of the Jews. [11] The king said to Haman, "The silver is given to you [to keep], and the people, [as well,] to do with them as you please".

יב וַיִּקָּרְאוּ סֹפְרֵי הַמֶּלֶךְ בַּחֹדֶשׁ הָרִאשׁוֹן בִּשְׁלוֹשָׁה עָשָׂר יוֹם בּוֹ וַיִּכָּתֵב כְּכָל אֲשֶׁר צִוָּה הָמָן אֶל אֲחַשְׁדַּרְפְּנֵי הַמֶּלֶךְ וְאֶל הַפַּחוֹת אֲשֶׁר עַל מְדִינָה וּמְדִינָה וְאֶל שָׂרֵי עַם וָעָם מְדִינָה וּמְדִינָה כִּכְתָבָהּ וְעַם וָעָם כִּלְשׁוֹנוֹ בְּשֵׁם הַמֶּלֶךְ אֲחַשְׁוֵרֹשׁ נִכְתָּב וְנֶחְתָּם בְּטַבַּעַת הַמֶּלֶךְ: יג וְנִשְׁלוֹחַ סְפָרִים בְּיַד הָרָצִים אֶל כָּל מְדִינוֹת הַמֶּלֶךְ לְהַשְׁמִיד לַהֲרֹג וּלְאַבֵּד אֶת כָּל הַיְּהוּדִים מִנַּעַר וְעַד זָקֵן טַף וְנָשִׁים בְּיוֹם

[12] The king's scribes were then summoned in the first month, on the thirteenth day of [the month], and whatever Haman commanded the king's satraps and governors who [ruled] over each state, and the ministers of each people, was written down; [to] each state according to its [form of] script, and [to] each people according to its language. It was written in the name of King Achashverosh and sealed with the king's signet ring. [13] Bills [of law] were to be sent by runners to all the king's states, [ordering them] to destroy, kill and annihilate all the Jews, both young and old, children and women, on one day—the thirteenth of the twelfth month, the month of Adar—and to plunder their [property as] spoil. [14] The text of the document was to become law in every state [and] publicized to all the peoples, for [them]

אחד בשלושה עשר לחדש שנים עשר הוא חדש אדר ושללם לבוז: יד פתשגן הכתב להנתן דת בכל מדינה מדינה גלוי לכל העמים להיות עתדים ליום הזה: טו הרצים יצאו דחופים בדבר המלך והדת נתנה בשושן הבירה והמלך והמן ישבו לשתות והעיר שושן נבוכה:

ד א ומרדכי ידע את כל אשר נעשה ויקרע מרדכי את בגדיו וילבש שק ואפר ויצא בתוך העיר ויזעק זעקה גדלה ומרה: ב ויבוא עד לפני שער המלך כי אין לבוא אל שער המלך בלבוש שק: ג ובכל מדינה ומדינה מקום אשר דבר המלך ודתו מגיע אבל גדול ליהודים וצום ובכי ומספד שק ואפר יצע לרבים: ד ותבואינה נערות אסתר וסריסיה ויגידו לה ותתחלחל המלכה מאד ותשלח בגדים להלביש את מרדכי ולהסיר שקו מעליו ולא קבל: ה ותקרא אסתר להתך מסריסי המלך אשר העמיד לפניה ותצוהו על מרדכי לדעת מה זה ועל מה זה: ו ויצא התך אל מרדכי אל רחוב העיר אשר לפני שער המלך: ז ויגד לו מרדכי את כל אשר קרהו ואת פרשת הכסף אשר אמר המן לשקול על גנזי המלך ביהודיים לאבדם: ח ואת פתשגן כתב הדת אשר נתן בשושן להשמידם נתן לו להראות את אסתר ולהגיד לה ולצוות עליה לבוא אל המלך להתחנן לו ולבקש מלפניו על עמה: ט ויבוא התך ויגד לאסתר את דברי מרדכי: י ותאמר אסתר להתך ותצוהו אל מרדכי: יא כל עבדי המלך ועם מדינות המלך יודעים אשר כל איש ואשה אשר יבוא אל המלך אל החצר הפנימית אשר לא יקרא אחת דתו להמית לבד מאשר יושיט לו המלך את שרביט הזהב וחיה ואני לא נקראתי לבוא אל המלך זה שלושים יום: יב ויגידו למרדכי את דברי אסתר: יג ויאמר מרדכי להשיב אל אסתר אל תדמי בנפשך להמלט בית המלך מכל היהודים: יד כי אם החרש תחרישי בעת הזאת רוח והצלה יעמוד ליהודים ממקום אחר ואת ובית אביך תאבדו ומי יודע אם לעת כזאת הגעת למלכות:

to be prepared for this day. ¹⁵The runners set out in haste with the king's decree and the law was published in Shushan the capital. The king and Haman then sat down to drink, while [the Jews of] the city of Shushan [were] bewildered.

4 ¹MORDECHAI, [however,] was aware of everything that had happened, so Mordechai tore his clothes and put on sackcloth and ashes. He then went out in the center of the city and let out a great and bitter cry. ²He came [only] as far as the front of the king's [palace] gate, for one did not enter the king's [palace] gate with sackcloth clothing. ³And in every state, wherever the king's decree reached and his law [took effect], there was great mourning for the Jews, with fasting, weeping and lamenting; sackcloth and ashes were worn by many. ⁴Esther's maids and attendants came and told her [about Mordechai,] and the queen was extremely shocked. She sent clothes to dress Mordechai [properly so that he may] remove his sackcloth, but he did not accept [them]. ⁵Esther then summoned Hasach, [one] of the king's attendants whom he appointed to be before her, and she instructed him about Mordechai, to find out [for] what was this [weeping], and why [he did not accept the clothes]. ⁶Hasach went out to Mordechai, to the [main] city square which was in front of the king's [palace] gate. ⁷Mordechai told him everything that had happened to him, and [about] the setting aside of the money—that Haman had said [he would have the money] weighed out for the king's treasuries in [exchange for] the Jews, so as to annihilate them. ⁸And he gave him the text of the document of law that was issued in Shushan to destroy [the Jews], to show [it] to Esther and to tell her [what had happened], and to order her to go to the king to entreat him and beseech him on behalf of her people. ⁹Hasach went and told Esther, Mordechai's words. ¹⁰Esther then said to Hasach, and instructed him to [tell] Mordechai, ¹¹"All the king's servants and the people of the king's states know, that any man or woman who comes to the king, to the inner courtyard, without being called, there is one law for him: to be put to death; only he to whom the king stretches out the golden scepter will live. I, [however,] have not been called to come to the king for the past thirty days." ¹²They then told Mordechai what Esther had said. ¹³Mordechai then told [them] to convey to Esther, "Do not imagine [you can] save yourself in the king's palace from [the fate of] all the Jews. ¹⁴For if you indeed keep silent at this time, relief and salvation will come to the Jews from another source, and you and your father's household will perish. And who knows if in a year's time you will hold the same royal position?!"

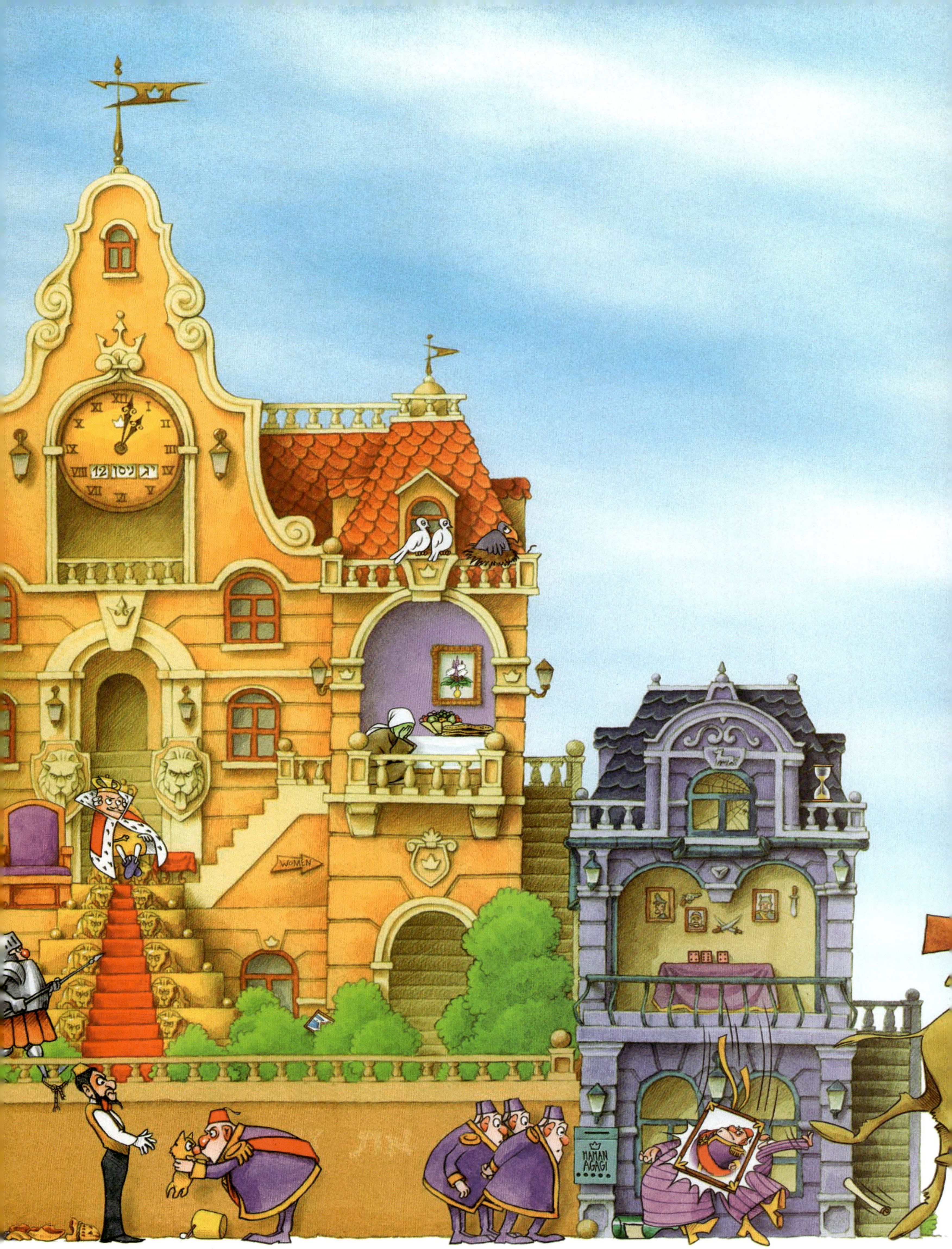

28

טו וַתֹּאמֶר אֶסְתֵּר לְהָשִׁיב אֶל מָרְדֳּכָי: טז לֵךְ כְּנוֹס אֶת כָּל הַיְּהוּדִים הַנִּמְצְאִים בְּשׁוּשָׁן וְצוּמוּ עָלַי וְאַל תֹּאכְלוּ וְאַל תִּשְׁתּוּ שְׁלֹשֶׁת יָמִים לַיְלָה וָיוֹם גַּם אֲנִי וְנַעֲרֹתַי אָצוּם כֵּן וּבְכֵן אָבוֹא אֶל הַמֶּלֶךְ אֲשֶׁר לֹא כַדָּת וְכַאֲשֶׁר אָבַדְתִּי אָבָדְתִּי: יז וַיַּעֲבֹר מָרְדֳּכָי וַיַּעַשׂ כְּכֹל אֲשֶׁר צִוְּתָה עָלָיו אֶסְתֵּר:

[15] Esther then told [them] to convey to Mordechai, [16] "Go [and] congregate all the Jews located in Shushan, and [proclaim a] fast on my behalf, that you will not eat and drink for three days, night and day. I, with my maids, will also fast in this way. And thus I will go to the king, [though] it is against the law, and just as I have [begun this way] to destruction, so will I [continue this way] to destruction." [17] Mordechai [thus] transgressed [GOD's commandment] and did according to everything that Esther instructed him.

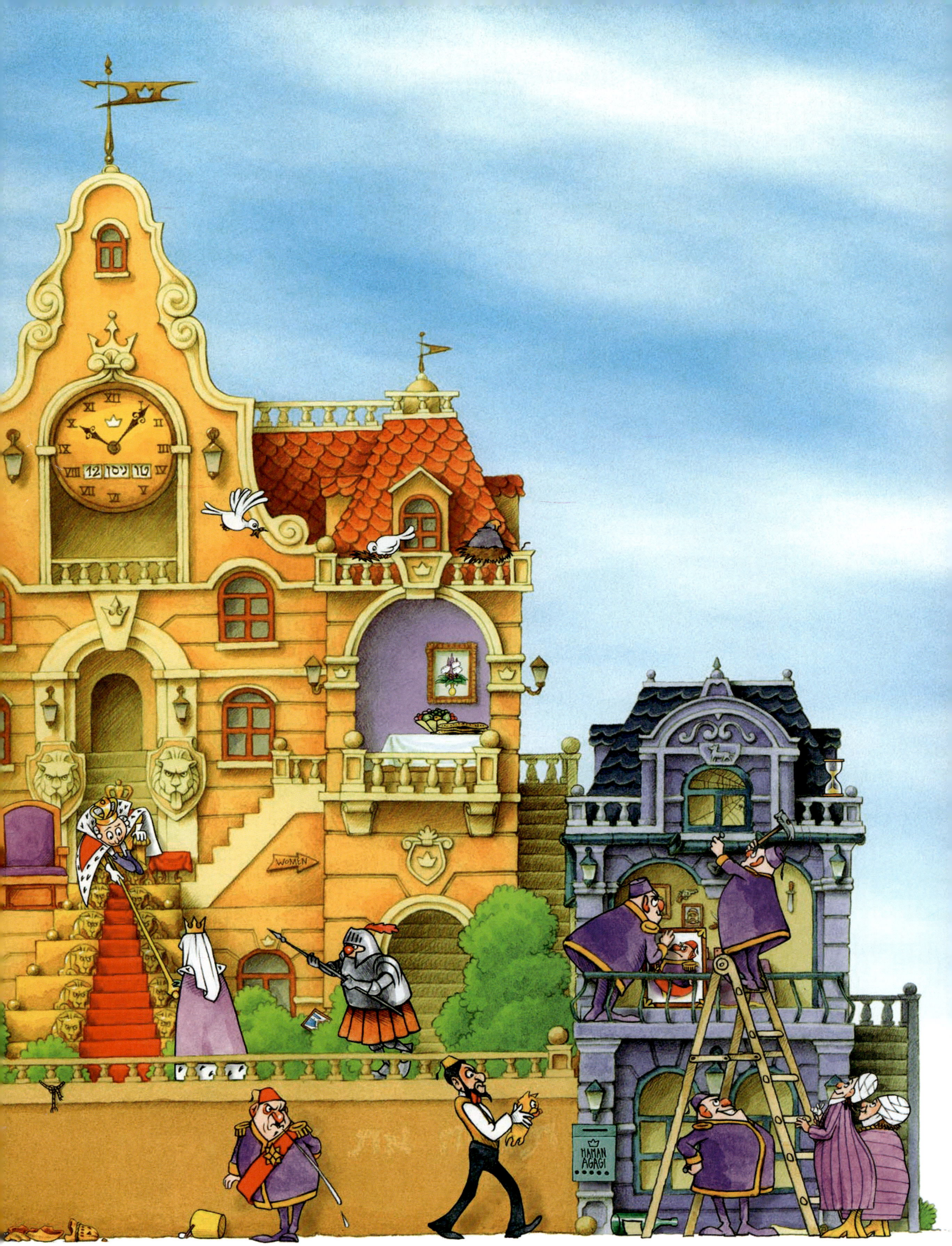

30

ה א וַיְהִי בַּיּוֹם הַשְּׁלִישִׁי וַתִּלְבַּשׁ אֶסְתֵּר מַלְכוּת וַתַּעֲמֹד בַּחֲצַר בֵּית הַמֶּלֶךְ הַפְּנִימִית נֹכַח בֵּית הַמֶּלֶךְ וְהַמֶּלֶךְ יוֹשֵׁב עַל כִּסֵּא מַלְכוּתוֹ בְּבֵית הַמַּלְכוּת נֹכַח פֶּתַח הַבָּיִת: ב וַיְהִי כִרְאוֹת הַמֶּלֶךְ אֶת אֶסְתֵּר הַמַּלְכָּה עֹמֶדֶת בֶּחָצֵר נָשְׂאָה חֵן בְּעֵינָיו וַיּוֹשֶׁט הַמֶּלֶךְ לְאֶסְתֵּר אֶת שַׁרְבִיט הַזָּהָב אֲשֶׁר בְּיָדוֹ וַתִּקְרַב אֶסְתֵּר וַתִּגַּע בְּרֹאשׁ הַשַּׁרְבִיט: ג וַיֹּאמֶר לָהּ הַמֶּלֶךְ מַה לָּךְ אֶסְתֵּר הַמַּלְכָּה וּמַה בַּקָּשָׁתֵךְ עַד חֲצִי הַמַּלְכוּת וְיִנָּתֵן לָךְ: ד וַתֹּאמֶר אֶסְתֵּר אִם עַל הַמֶּלֶךְ טוֹב יָבוֹא הַמֶּלֶךְ וְהָמָן הַיּוֹם אֶל הַמִּשְׁתֶּה אֲשֶׁר עָשִׂיתִי לוֹ: ה וַיֹּאמֶר הַמֶּלֶךְ מַהֲרוּ אֶת הָמָן לַעֲשׂוֹת אֶת דְּבַר אֶסְתֵּר וַיָּבֹא הַמֶּלֶךְ וְהָמָן אֶל הַמִּשְׁתֶּה אֲשֶׁר עָשְׂתָה אֶסְתֵּר:

5 [1] THEN, ON THE THIRD DAY, Esther put on [her] royal [robes] and stood in the inner courtyard of the king's palace, directly facing the king's chamber, while the king was sitting on his royal throne in the royal chamber, facing the entrance of the chamber. [2] Then, when the king saw Queen Esther standing in the courtyard, she carried charm before him, and the king stretched out the golden scepter in his hand to Esther. Esther then approached and touched the tip of the scepter. [3] The king then said to her, "Queen Esther, what do you want and what is your wish? [You may ask for] even half the kingdom and it will be granted you." [4] Esther replied, "If it pleases the king, may the king, with Haman, come today to the feast that I have prepared for him." [5] The king then said, "Quickly bring Haman to carry out what Esther has said," and [so] the king and Haman came to the feast that Esther had prepared.

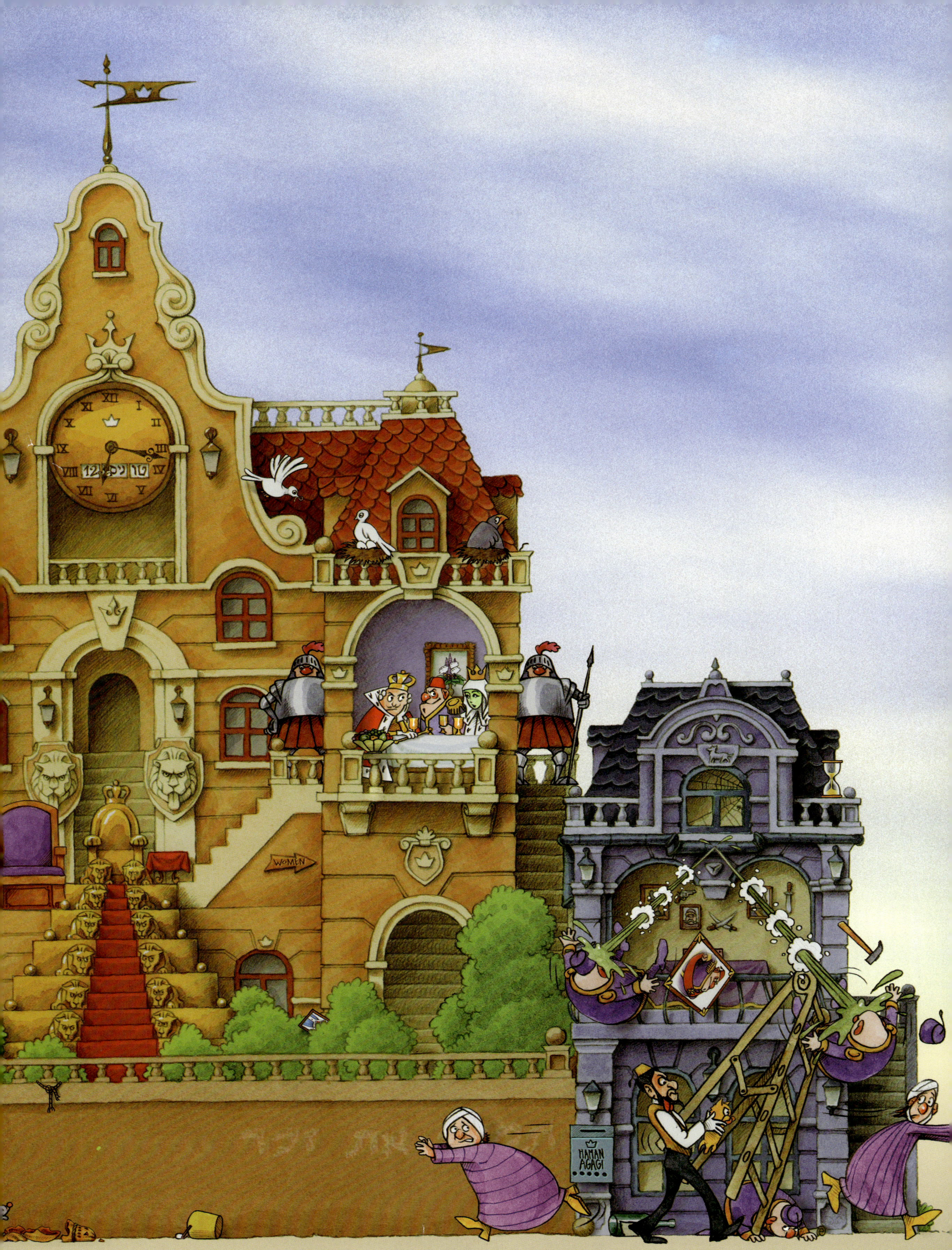

32

ו וַיֹּאמֶר הַמֶּלֶךְ לְאֶסְתֵּר בְּמִשְׁתֵּה הַיַּיִן מַה שְּׁאֵלָתֵךְ וְיִנָּתֵן לָךְ וּמַה בַּקָּשָׁתֵךְ עַד חֲצִי הַמַּלְכוּת וְתֵעָשׂ: ז וַתַּעַן אֶסְתֵּר וַתֹּאמַר שְׁאֵלָתִי וּבַקָּשָׁתִי: ח אִם מָצָאתִי חֵן בְּעֵינֵי הַמֶּלֶךְ וְאִם עַל הַמֶּלֶךְ טוֹב לָתֵת אֶת שְׁאֵלָתִי וְלַעֲשׂוֹת אֶת בַּקָּשָׁתִי יָבוֹא הַמֶּלֶךְ וְהָמָן אֶל הַמִּשְׁתֶּה אֲשֶׁר אֶעֱשֶׂה לָהֶם וּמָחָר אֶעֱשֶׂה כִּדְבַר הַמֶּלֶךְ:

[6] The king said to Esther at the wine feast, "What is your request and it will be granted you? And what is your wish? [You may ask for] even half the kingdom and [your wish] will be fulfilled." [7] Esther responded and said, "[This is] my request and my wish. [8] If the king regards me favorably, and if it pleases the king to fulfill my request and to carry out my wish, may the king, with Haman, come to the feast that I shall prepare for them, and tomorrow I shall carry out what the king has [asked]."

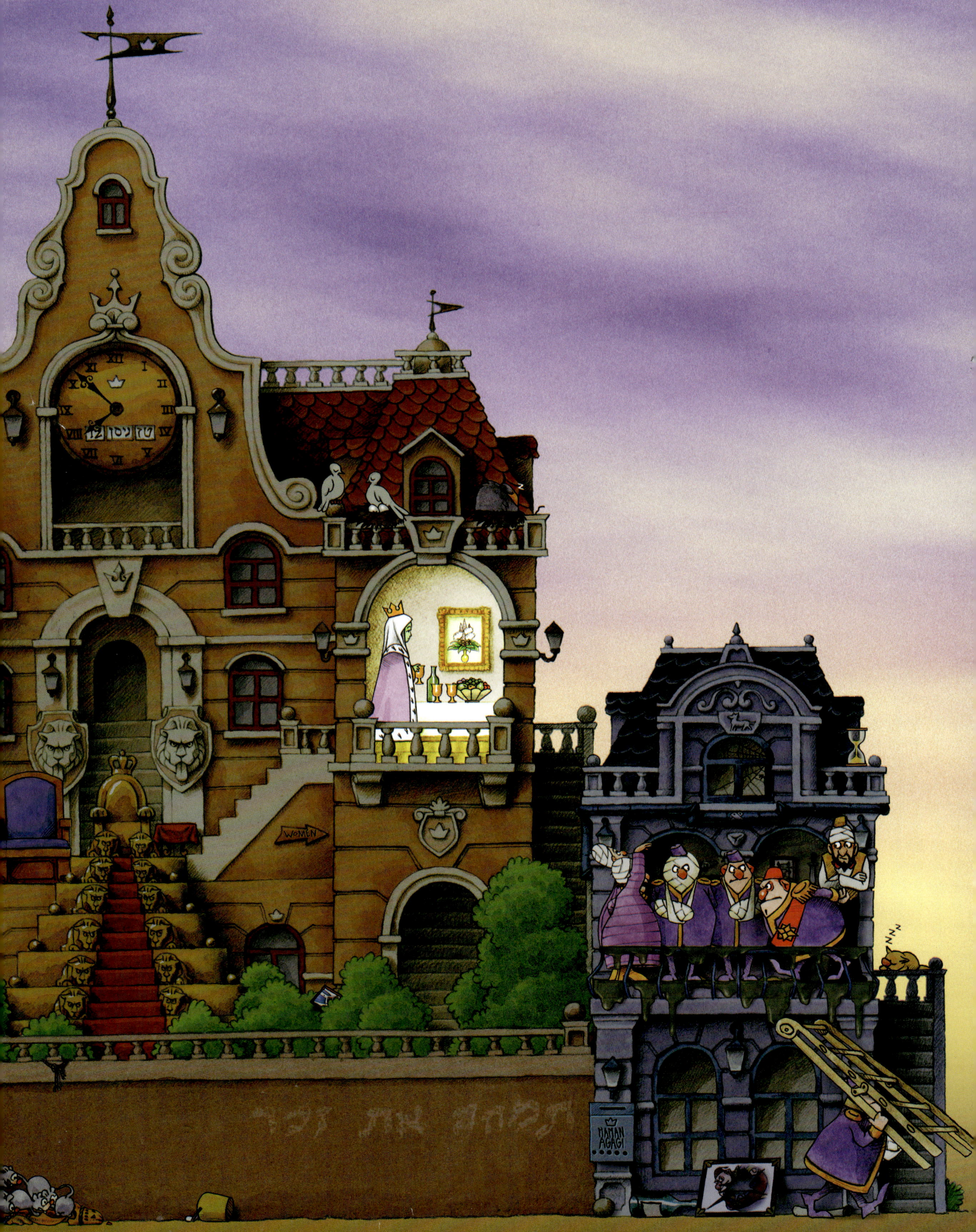

34

ט וַיֵּצֵא הָמָן בַּיּוֹם הַהוּא שָׂמֵחַ וְטוֹב לֵב וְכִרְאוֹת הָמָן אֶת מָרְדֳּכַי בְּשַׁעַר הַמֶּלֶךְ וְלֹא קָם וְלֹא זָע מִמֶּנּוּ וַיִּמָּלֵא הָמָן עַל מָרְדֳּכַי חֵמָה: י וַיִּתְאַפַּק הָמָן וַיָּבוֹא אֶל בֵּיתוֹ וַיִּשְׁלַח וַיָּבֵא אֶת אֹהֲבָיו וְאֶת זֶרֶשׁ אִשְׁתּוֹ: יא וַיְסַפֵּר לָהֶם הָמָן אֶת כְּבוֹד עָשְׁרוֹ וְרֹב בָּנָיו וְאֵת כָּל אֲשֶׁר גִּדְּלוֹ הַמֶּלֶךְ וְאֵת אֲשֶׁר נִשְּׂאוֹ עַל הַשָּׂרִים וְעַבְדֵי הַמֶּלֶךְ: יב וַיֹּאמֶר הָמָן אַף לֹא הֵבִיאָה אֶסְתֵּר הַמַּלְכָּה עִם הַמֶּלֶךְ אֶל הַמִּשְׁתֶּה אֲשֶׁר עָשָׂתָה כִּי אִם אוֹתִי וְגַם לְמָחָר אֲנִי קָרוּא לָהּ עִם הַמֶּלֶךְ: יג וְכָל זֶה אֵינֶנּוּ שֹׁוֶה לִי בְּכָל עֵת אֲשֶׁר אֲנִי רֹאֶה אֶת מָרְדֳּכַי הַיְּהוּדִי יוֹשֵׁב בְּשַׁעַר הַמֶּלֶךְ:

[9] Haman left [the king] on that day happy and in good spirits, but when Haman saw Mordechai at the king's [palace] gate, and he did not rise or [even] move [out of respect] for him, Haman was filled with rage against Mordechai. [10] Haman restrained himself and came to his house. He then sent for and brought [together] his friends and Zeresh, his wife. [11] Haman told them about the honor [he received from] his wealth, and about his great number of children, and how the king had promoted him and raised his position over the ministers and the king's servants. [12] Haman then said, "Even Queen Esther did not bring anyone [else] with the king, except me, to the feast she prepared, and tomorrow, as well, I am invited to her [feast] with the king. [13] All this, [however,] is worth nothing to me, every time I see Mordechai the Jew sitting at the king's [palace] gate!"

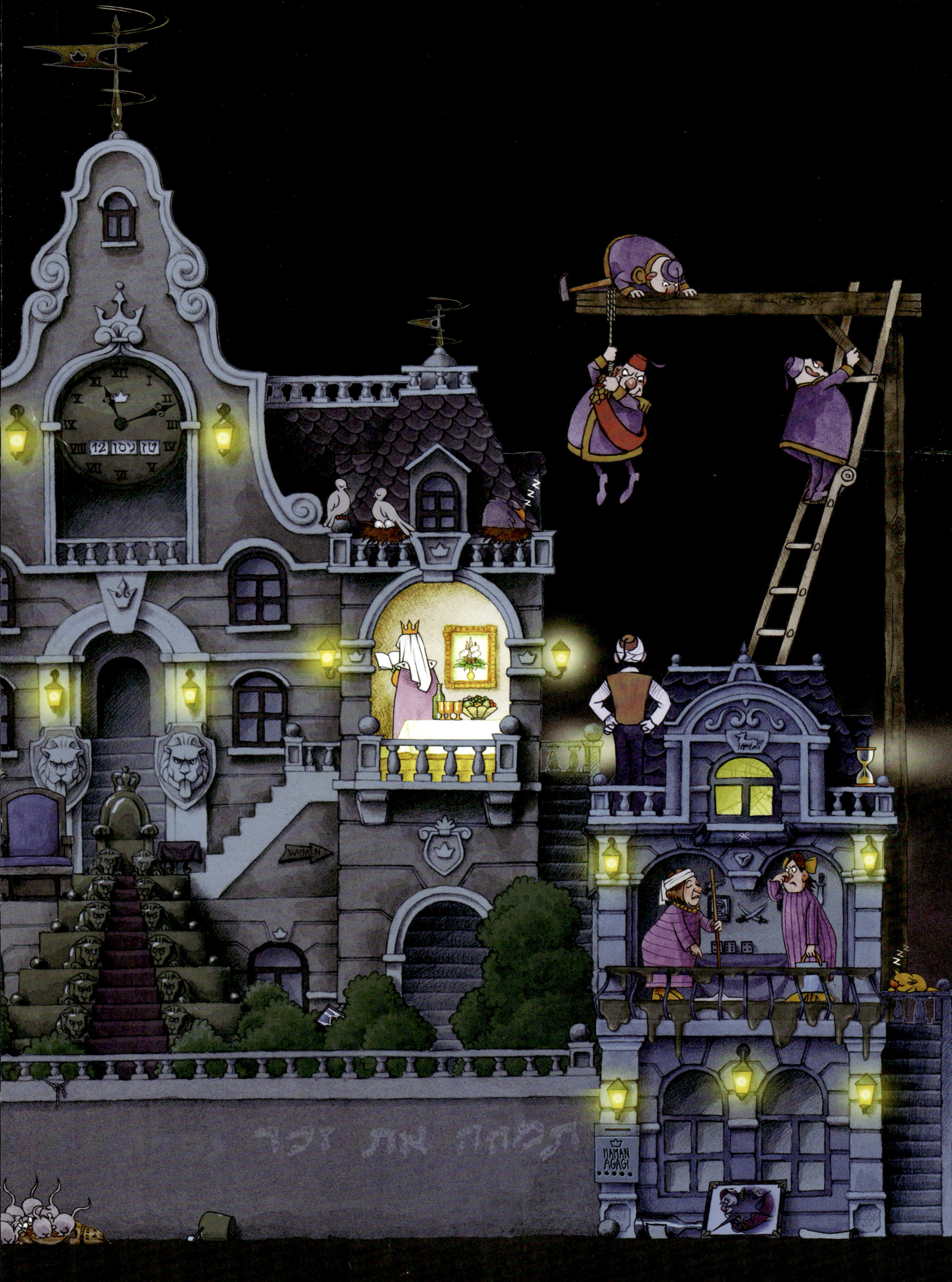
טז ניסן 12
WOMEN
תמחה את זכר
HAMAN AGAGI

¹⁴ Zeresh his wife, with all his friends, then said to him, "Let [the workers] make a gallows fifty cubits high, and in the morning tell the king [about it], and they shall hang Mordechai on it; and [then] go with the king to the feast feeling happy!" The idea pleased Haman and he made the gallows.

6 ¹ THAT NIGHT, sleep eluded the king, so he asked to have the record book of the chronicles brought [before him], and they were read out before the king. ² [There] it was found written that Mordechai had told about Bigsana and Teresh, two of the king's attendants, of the guards of the inner court, who had conspired to act against King Achashverosh. ³ The king then asked, "What honor or [mark of] greatness was [given] to Mordechai for this?" The king's young men, his servants, answered, "Nothing was done for him."

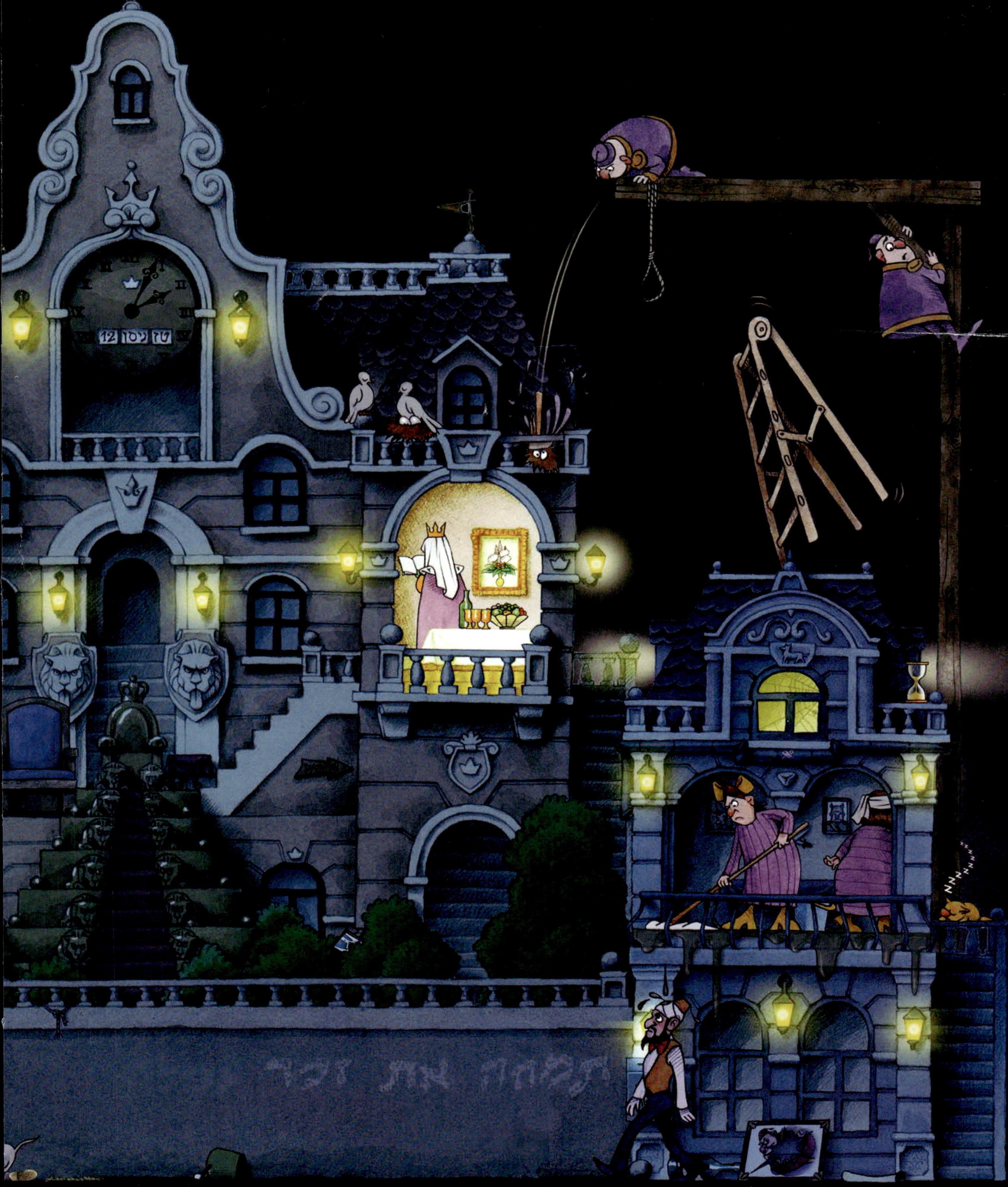

טז נסן 12

ד וַיֹּאמֶר הַמֶּלֶךְ מִי בֶחָצֵר וְהָמָן בָּא לַחֲצַר בֵּית־הַמֶּלֶךְ הַחִיצוֹנָה לֵאמֹר לַמֶּלֶךְ לִתְלוֹת אֶת־מָרְדֳּכַי עַל־הָעֵץ אֲשֶׁר־הֵכִין לוֹ: ה וַיֹּאמְרוּ נַעֲרֵי הַמֶּלֶךְ אֵלָיו הִנֵּה הָמָן עֹמֵד בֶּחָצֵר וַיֹּאמֶר הַמֶּלֶךְ יָבוֹא: ו וַיָּבוֹא הָמָן וַיֹּאמֶר לוֹ הַמֶּלֶךְ מַה־לַּעֲשׂוֹת בָּאִישׁ אֲשֶׁר הַמֶּלֶךְ חָפֵץ בִּיקָרוֹ וַיֹּאמֶר הָמָן בְּלִבּוֹ לְמִי יַחְפֹּץ הַמֶּלֶךְ לַעֲשׂוֹת יְקָר יוֹתֵר מִמֶּנִּי: ז וַיֹּאמֶר הָמָן אֶל־הַמֶּלֶךְ אִישׁ אֲשֶׁר הַמֶּלֶךְ חָפֵץ בִּיקָרוֹ: ח יָבִיאוּ לְבוּשׁ מַלְכוּת אֲשֶׁר לָבַשׁ־בּוֹ הַמֶּלֶךְ וְסוּס אֲשֶׁר רָכַב עָלָיו הַמֶּלֶךְ וַאֲשֶׁר נִתַּן כֶּתֶר מַלְכוּת בְּרֹאשׁוֹ: ט וְנָתוֹן הַלְּבוּשׁ וְהַסּוּס עַל־יַד־אִישׁ מִשָּׂרֵי הַמֶּלֶךְ הַפַּרְתְּמִים וְהִלְבִּישׁוּ אֶת־הָאִישׁ אֲשֶׁר הַמֶּלֶךְ חָפֵץ בִּיקָרוֹ וְהִרְכִּיבֻהוּ עַל־הַסּוּס בִּרְחוֹב הָעִיר וְקָרְאוּ לְפָנָיו כָּכָה יֵעָשֶׂה לָאִישׁ אֲשֶׁר הַמֶּלֶךְ חָפֵץ בִּיקָרוֹ: י וַיֹּאמֶר הַמֶּלֶךְ לְהָמָן מַהֵר קַח אֶת־הַלְּבוּשׁ וְאֶת־הַסּוּס כַּאֲשֶׁר דִּבַּרְתָּ וַעֲשֵׂה־כֵן לְמָרְדֳּכַי הַיְּהוּדִי הַיּוֹשֵׁב בְּשַׁעַר הַמֶּלֶךְ אַל־תַּפֵּל דָּבָר מִכֹּל אֲשֶׁר דִּבַּרְתָּ:

The king then asked, "Who is in the courtyard?" and [just then] Haman had come to the inner palace courtyard, to tell the king [his wish] to hang Mordechai on the gallows that he had prepared for him. [5] The king's young men answered [the king], " It is Haman standing in the courtyard." The king said, " Let him enter!" [6] Haman entered, and the king asked him, " What should be done for the man whom the king wishes to honor?" Haman thought to himself," Who would the king wish to honor more than me?!" [7] So Haman said to the king, "A man whom the king wishes to honor — [8] let [the king's servants] bring the royal robes which the king wore, and the horse on which the king rode [at his coronation], and the royal crown that was [then] placed on his head. [9] Let the robes and the horse then be given under the supervision of one of the king's ministers, [one] of the governors, and [the king's servants] shall dress the man whom the king wishes to honor [in the royal robes], and ride him on the horse in the [main] city square. They shall call out before him, ' This is what is done to the man whom the king wishes to honor!' " [10] The king then said to Haman, "Quickly take the robes and the horse, as you said, and do this for Mordechai the Jew who sits at the king's [palace] gate. Do not omit anything of whatever you said!"

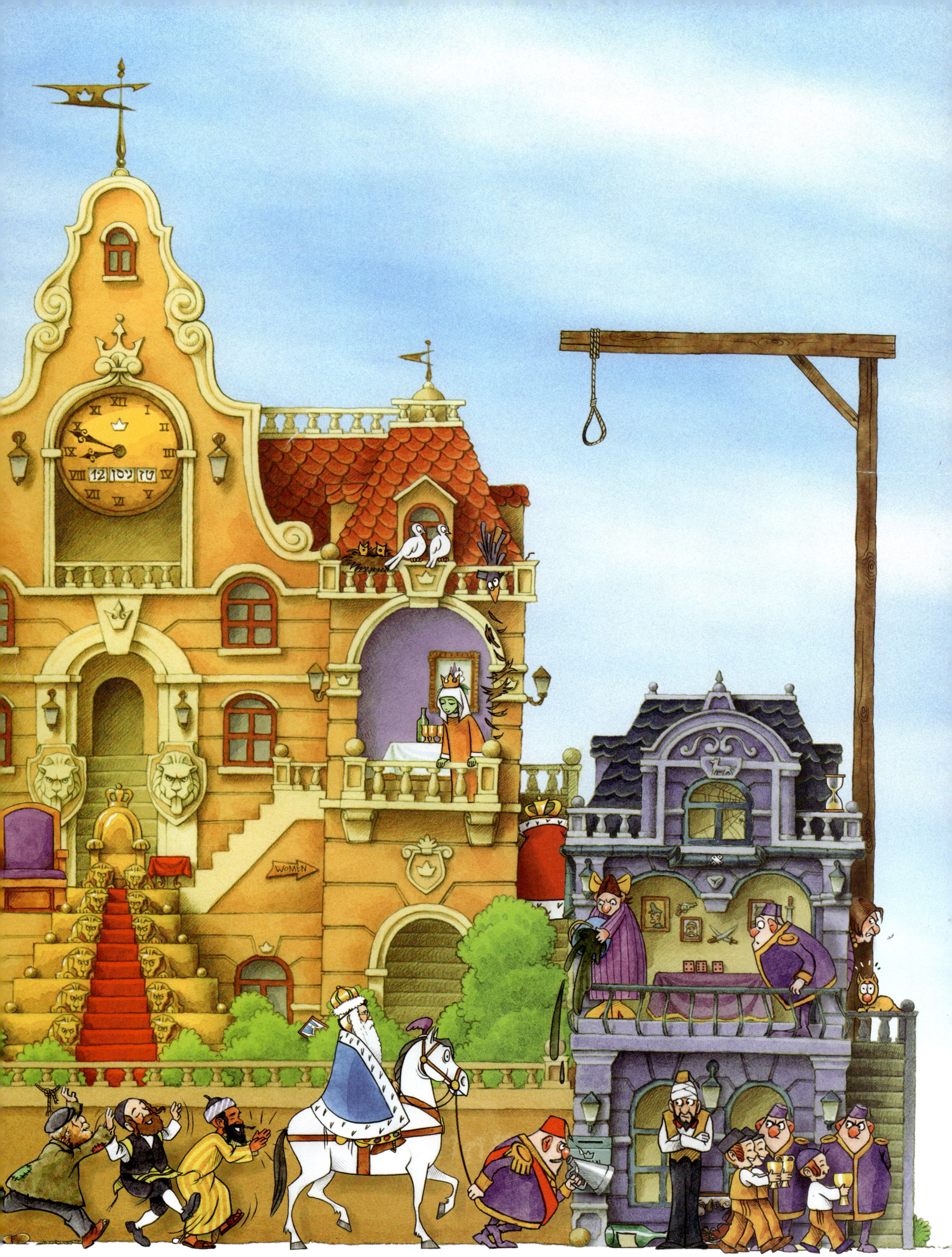

טז ניסן 12
WOMEN

יא וַיִּקַּח הָמָן אֶת הַלְּבוּשׁ וְאֶת הַסּוּס וַיַּלְבֵּשׁ אֶת מָרְדֳּכָי וַיַּרְכִּיבֵהוּ בִּרְחוֹב הָעִיר וַיִּקְרָא לְפָנָיו כָּכָה יֵעָשֶׂה לָאִישׁ אֲשֶׁר הַמֶּלֶךְ חָפֵץ בִּיקָרוֹ:

[11] Haman took the robes and the horse and dressed Mordechai [in the robes]. He then rode him in the [main] city square and called out before him, "This is what is done to the man whom the king wishes to honor!"

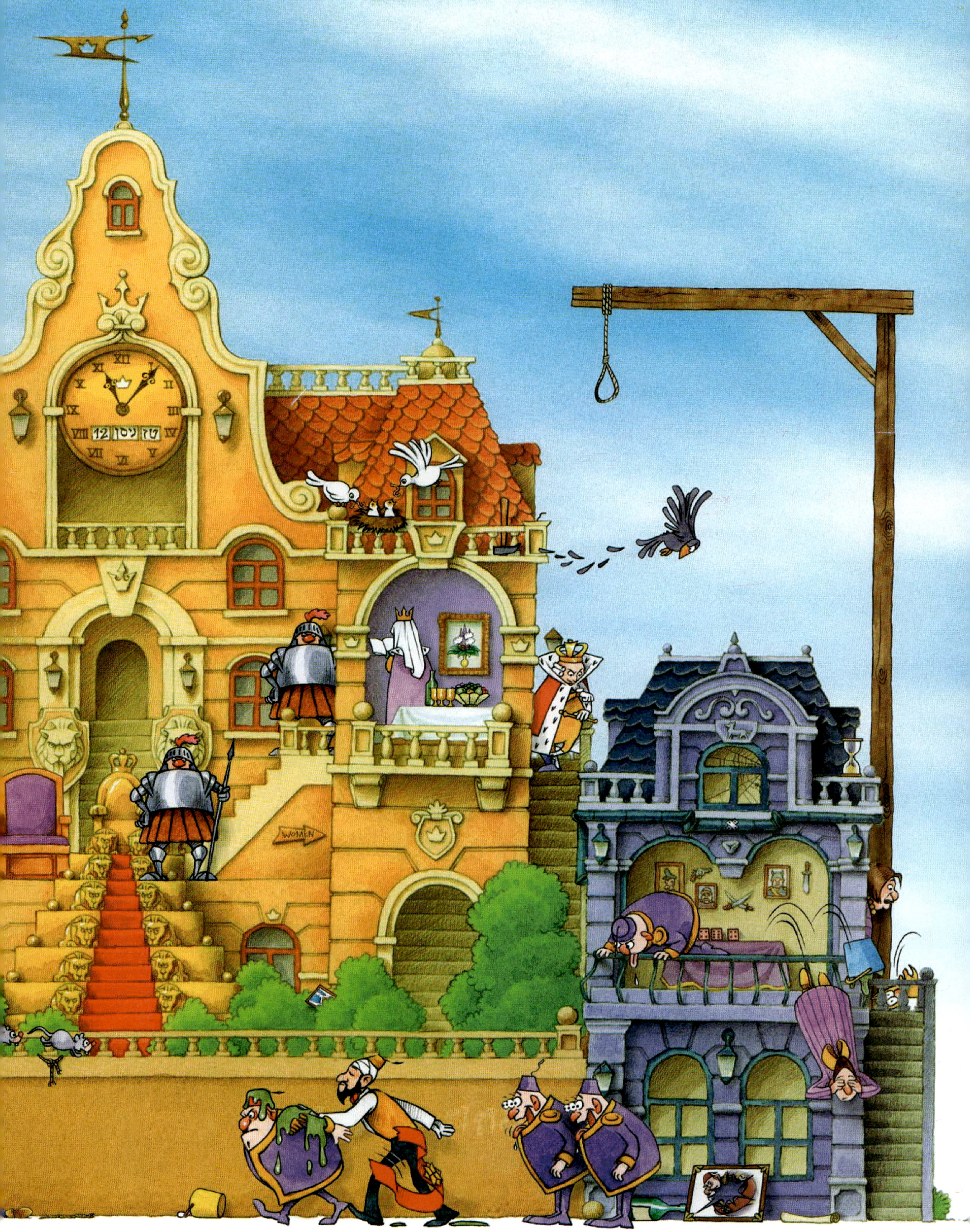

42

יג וַיָּשָׁב מָרְדֳּכַי אֶל שַׁעַר הַמֶּלֶךְ וְהָמָן נִדְחַף אֶל בֵּיתוֹ אָבֵל וַחֲפוּי רֹאשׁ: יג וַיְסַפֵּר הָמָן לְזֶרֶשׁ אִשְׁתּוֹ וּלְכָל אֹהֲבָיו אֵת כָּל אֲשֶׁר קָרָהוּ וַיֹּאמְרוּ לוֹ חֲכָמָיו וְזֶרֶשׁ אִשְׁתּוֹ אִם מִזֶּרַע הַיְּהוּדִים מָרְדֳּכַי אֲשֶׁר הַחִלּוֹתָ לִנְפֹּל לְפָנָיו לֹא תוּכַל לוֹ כִּי נָפוֹל תִּפּוֹל לְפָנָיו: יד עוֹדָם מְדַבְּרִים עִמּוֹ וְסָרִיסֵי הַמֶּלֶךְ הִגִּיעוּ וַיַּבְהִלוּ לְהָבִיא אֶת הָמָן אֶל הַמִּשְׁתֶּה אֲשֶׁר עָשְׂתָה אֶסְתֵּר:

[12] Mordechai then returned to the king's [palace] gate, while Haman hurried to his house, in mourning and his head covered [in dirt]. [13] Haman then told Zeresh, his wife, and all his friends everything that had happened to him. His wise men and Zeresh, his wife, said to him, "If Mordechai, before whom you have begun to fall, is a descendant of the Jews, you will not be able [to harm] him, for you will surely fall before him." [14] They were still speaking with him when the king's attendants arrived, and they rushed to bring Haman to the feast that Esther had prepared.

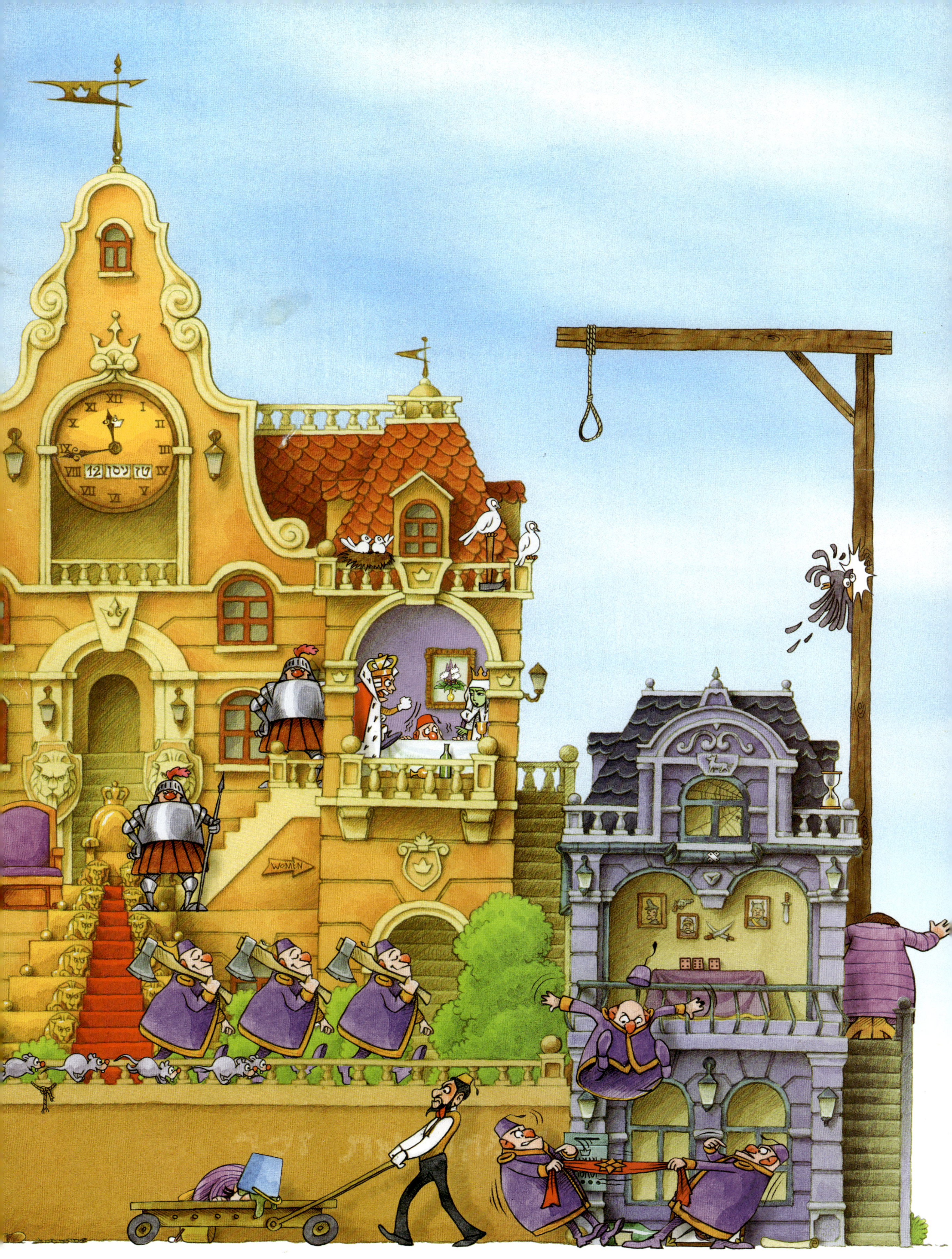

WOMEN

ז ״ וַיָּבֹא הַמֶּלֶךְ וְהָמָן לִשְׁתּוֹת עִם אֶסְתֵּר הַמַּלְכָּה: ב וַיֹּאמֶר הַמֶּלֶךְ לְאֶסְתֵּר גַּם בַּיּוֹם הַשֵּׁנִי בְּמִשְׁתֵּה הַיַּיִן מַה שְּׁאֵלָתֵךְ אֶסְתֵּר הַמַּלְכָּה וְתִנָּתֵן לָךְ וּמַה בַּקָּשָׁתֵךְ עַד חֲצִי הַמַּלְכוּת וְתֵעָשׂ: ג וַתַּעַן אֶסְתֵּר הַמַּלְכָּה וַתֹּאמַר אִם מָצָאתִי חֵן בְּעֵינֶיךָ הַמֶּלֶךְ וְאִם עַל הַמֶּלֶךְ טוֹב תִּנָּתֶן לִי נַפְשִׁי בִּשְׁאֵלָתִי וְעַמִּי בְּבַקָּשָׁתִי: ד כִּי נִמְכַּרְנוּ אֲנִי וְעַמִּי לְהַשְׁמִיד לַהֲרוֹג וּלְאַבֵּד וְאִלּוּ לַעֲבָדִים וְלִשְׁפָחוֹת נִמְכַּרְנוּ הֶחֱרַשְׁתִּי כִּי אֵין הַצָּר שׁוֶֹה בְּנֵזֶק הַמֶּלֶךְ: ה וַיֹּאמֶר הַמֶּלֶךְ אֲחַשְׁוֵרוֹשׁ וַיֹּאמֶר לְאֶסְתֵּר הַמַּלְכָּה מִי הוּא זֶה וְאֵי זֶה הוּא אֲשֶׁר מְלָאוֹ לִבּוֹ לַעֲשׂוֹת כֵּן: ו וַתֹּאמֶר אֶסְתֵּר אִישׁ צַר וְאוֹיֵב הָמָן הָרָע הַזֶּה וְהָמָן נִבְעַת מִלִּפְנֵי הַמֶּלֶךְ וְהַמַּלְכָּה:

7 [1] THE KING AND HAMAN then came to drink with Queen Esther. [2] On the second day, as well, at the wine feast, the king asked Esther, "Queen Esther, what is your request and it will be granted you? And what is your wish? [You may ask for] even half the kingdom and [your wish] will be fulfilled." [3] Queen Esther responded and said, "If you regard me favorably, O king, and if it pleases the king, as my request let my life be granted, and as my wish, my people. [4] For I and my people have been sold to be destroyed, killed and annihilated. And if we were sold as slaves and maidservants I would have kept silent, but the oppressor is not concerned about the damage [caused to] the king." [5] King Achashverosh then said, [speaking directly] to Queen Esther, "Who is this and where is he, who dared to do this?!" [6] Esther replied, "An oppressor and enemy, this evil Haman!" Haman was then terrified before the king and the queen.

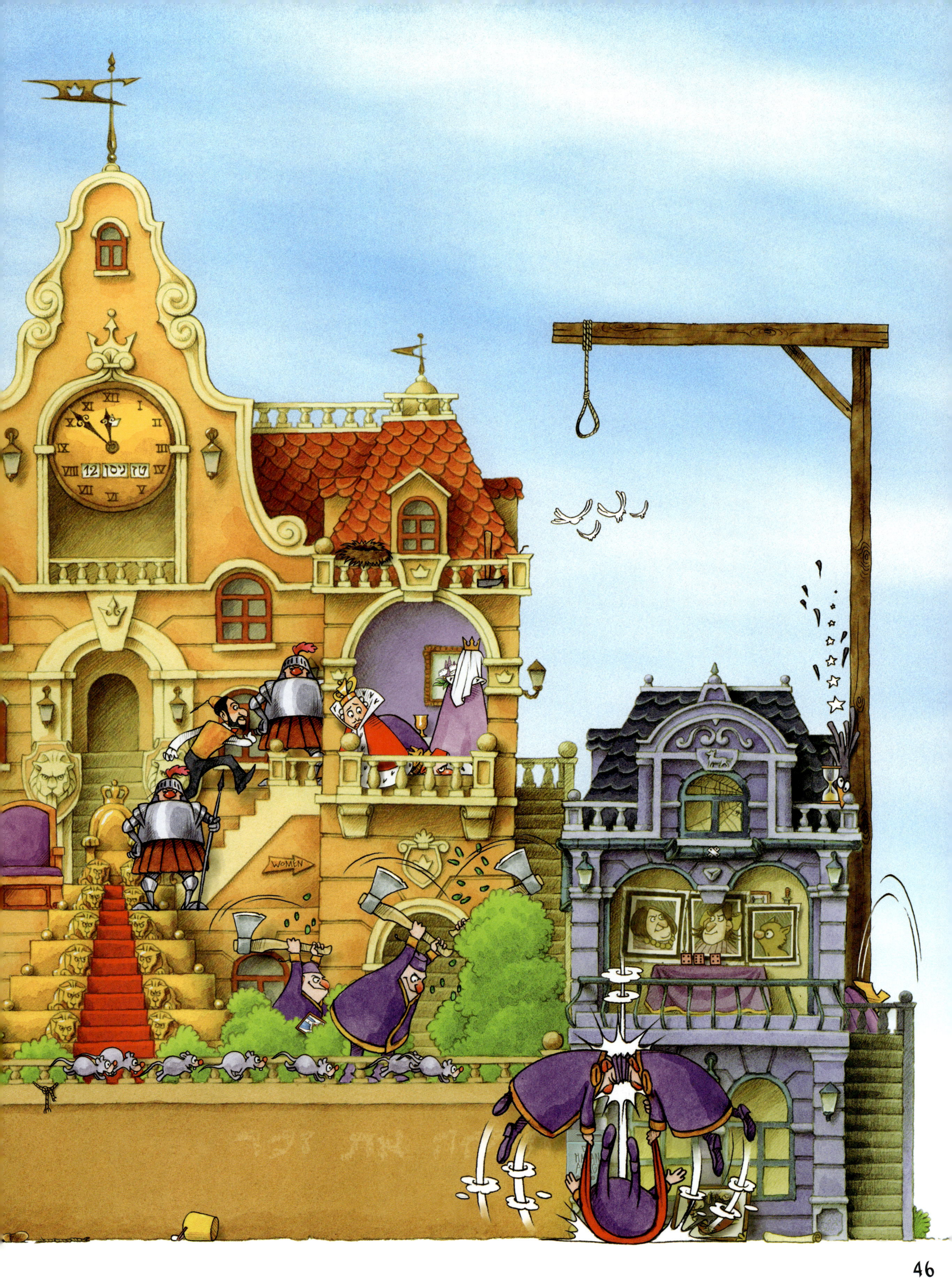
WOMEN

ז וְהַמֶּלֶךְ קָם בַּחֲמָתוֹ מִמִּשְׁתֵּה הַיַּיִן אֶל גִּנַּת הַבִּיתָן וְהָמָן עָמַד לְבַקֵּשׁ עַל נַפְשׁוֹ מֵאֶסְתֵּר הַמַּלְכָּה כִּי רָאָה כִּי כָלְתָה אֵלָיו הָרָעָה מֵאֵת הַמֶּלֶךְ:

[7] The king then got up from the wine feast in a rage, [and went out] to the garden orchard, while Haman stood up to plead for his life from Queen Esther, for he realized that the king's bad [feelings] towards him were absolute.

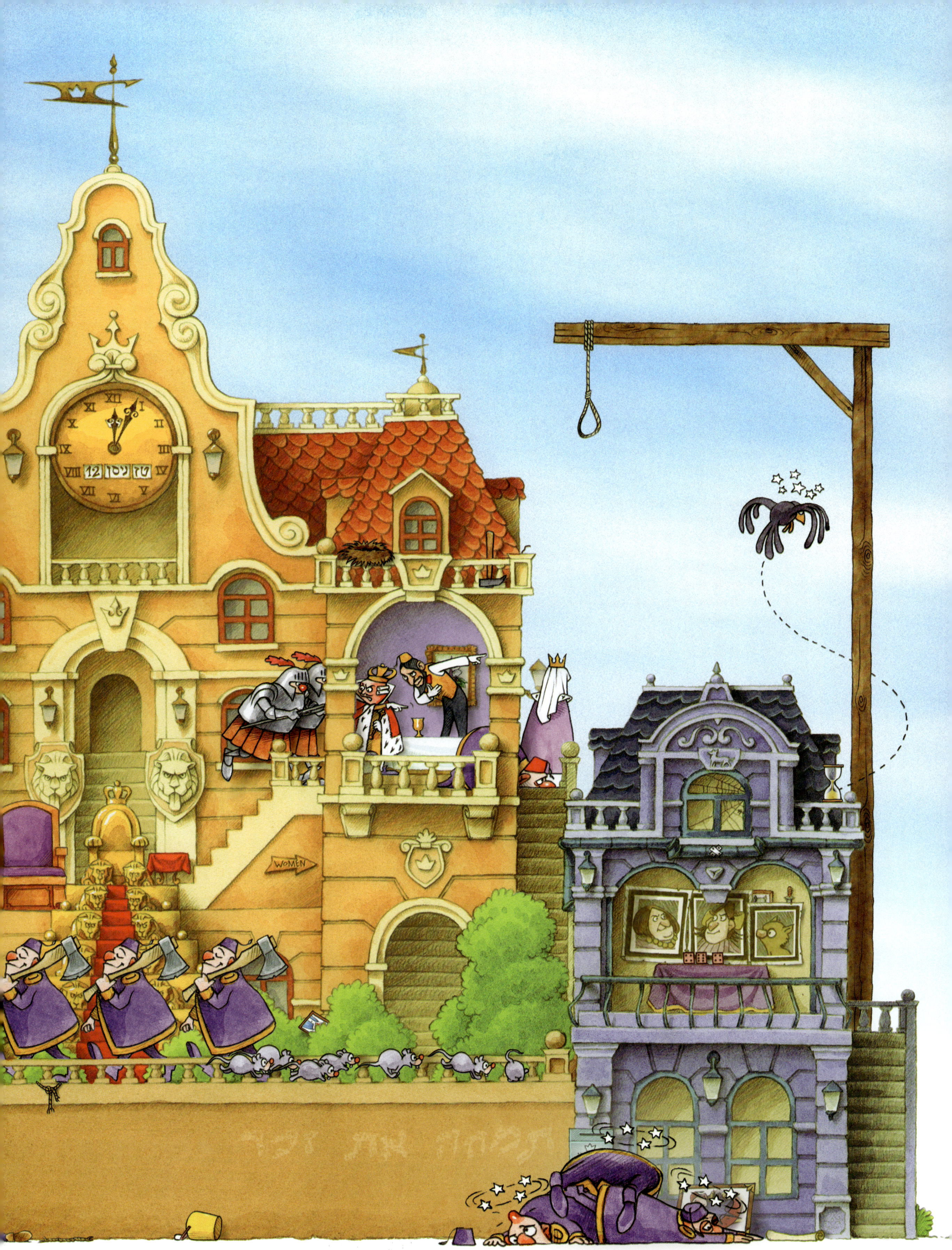

48

ח וְהַמֶּלֶךְ שָׁב מִגִּנַּת הַבִּיתָן אֶל בֵּית מִשְׁתֵּה הַיַּיִן וְהָמָן נֹפֵל עַל הַמִּטָּה אֲשֶׁר אֶסְתֵּר עָלֶיהָ וַיֹּאמֶר הַמֶּלֶךְ הֲגַם לִכְבּוֹשׁ אֶת הַמַּלְכָּה עִמִּי בַּבָּיִת הַדָּבָר יָצָא מִפִּי הַמֶּלֶךְ וּפְנֵי הָמָן חָפוּ: ט וַיֹּאמֶר חַרְבוֹנָה אֶחָד מִן הַסָּרִיסִים לִפְנֵי הַמֶּלֶךְ גַּם הִנֵּה הָעֵץ אֲשֶׁר עָשָׂה הָמָן לְמָרְדֳּכַי אֲשֶׁר דִּבֶּר טוֹב עַל הַמֶּלֶךְ עֹמֵד בְּבֵית הָמָן גָּבֹהַּ חֲמִשִּׁים אַמָּה וַיֹּאמֶר הַמֶּלֶךְ תְּלֻהוּ עָלָיו: י וַיִּתְלוּ אֶת הָמָן עַל הָעֵץ אֲשֶׁר הֵכִין לְמָרְדֳּכָי וַחֲמַת הַמֶּלֶךְ שָׁכָכָה:

[8] The king then returned from the garden orchard to the wine feast chamber, [as] Haman was falling on the couch on which Esther was [lying]. The king said, "Does [he] also [wish] to assault the queen in my presence [here] in the palace?!" The words had [hardly] left the king's mouth and [the king's servants] covered Haman's face. [9] Charvonah, one of the attendants, then said before the king, "There is also the gallows which Haman made for Mordechai, who spoke good things for the king, standing in Haman's house, fifty cubits high!" The king replied, "Hang him on it!" [10] So they hanged Haman on the gallows he had prepared for Mordechai, and the king's anger abated.

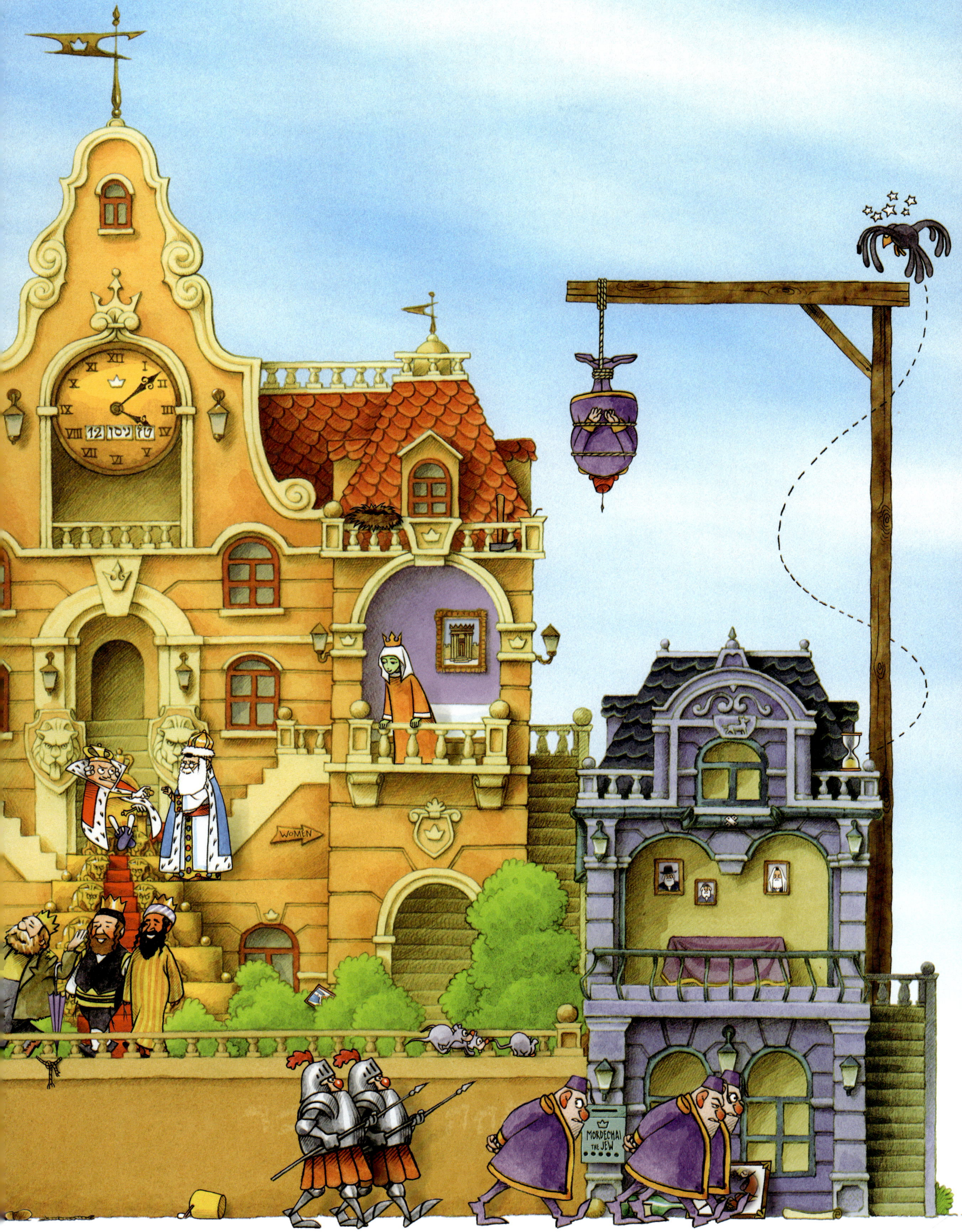

50

ח ס בַּיּוֹם הַהוּא נָתַן הַמֶּלֶךְ אֲחַשְׁוֵרוֹשׁ לְאֶסְתֵּר הַמַּלְכָּה אֶת־בֵּית הָמָן צֹרֵר הַיְּהוּדִיים וּמָרְדֳּכַי בָּא לִפְנֵי הַמֶּלֶךְ כִּי־הִגִּידָה אֶסְתֵּר מַה הוּא־לָהּ: ב וַיָּסַר הַמֶּלֶךְ אֶת־טַבַּעְתּוֹ אֲשֶׁר הֶעֱבִיר מֵהָמָן וַיִּתְּנָהּ לְמָרְדֳּכָי וַתָּשֶׂם אֶסְתֵּר אֶת־מָרְדֳּכַי עַל־בֵּית הָמָן: ג וַתּוֹסֶף אֶסְתֵּר וַתְּדַבֵּר לִפְנֵי הַמֶּלֶךְ וַתִּפֹּל לִפְנֵי רַגְלָיו וַתֵּבְךְּ וַתִּתְחַנֶּן־לוֹ לְהַעֲבִיר אֶת־רָעַת הָמָן הָאֲגָגִי וְאֵת מַחֲשַׁבְתּוֹ אֲשֶׁר חָשַׁב עַל־הַיְּהוּדִים: ד וַיּוֹשֶׁט הַמֶּלֶךְ לְאֶסְתֵּר אֵת שַׁרְבִט הַזָּהָב וַתָּקָם אֶסְתֵּר וַתַּעֲמֹד לִפְנֵי הַמֶּלֶךְ: ה וַתֹּאמֶר אִם־עַל־הַמֶּלֶךְ טוֹב וְאִם־מָצָאתִי חֵן לְפָנָיו וְכָשֵׁר הַדָּבָר לִפְנֵי הַמֶּלֶךְ וְטוֹבָה אֲנִי בְּעֵינָיו יִכָּתֵב לְהָשִׁיב אֶת־הַסְּפָרִים מַחֲשֶׁבֶת הָמָן בֶּן־הַמְּדָתָא הָאֲגָגִי אֲשֶׁר כָּתַב לְאַבֵּד אֶת־הַיְּהוּדִים אֲשֶׁר בְּכָל־מְדִינוֹת הַמֶּלֶךְ: ו כִּי אֵיכָכָה אוּכַל וְרָאִיתִי בָּרָעָה אֲשֶׁר־יִמְצָא אֶת־עַמִּי וְאֵיכָכָה אוּכַל וְרָאִיתִי בְּאָבְדַן מוֹלַדְתִּי: ז וַיֹּאמֶר הַמֶּלֶךְ אֲחַשְׁוֵרֹשׁ לְאֶסְתֵּר הַמַּלְכָּה וּלְמָרְדֳּכַי הַיְּהוּדִי הִנֵּה בֵית־הָמָן נָתַתִּי לְאֶסְתֵּר וְאֹתוֹ תָּלוּ עַל־הָעֵץ עַל אֲשֶׁר־שָׁלַח יָדוֹ בַּיְּהוּדִיים: ח וְאַתֶּם כִּתְבוּ עַל־הַיְּהוּדִים כַּטּוֹב בְּעֵינֵיכֶם בְּשֵׁם הַמֶּלֶךְ וְחִתְמוּ בְּטַבַּעַת הַמֶּלֶךְ כִּי־כְתָב אֲשֶׁר־נִכְתָּב בְּשֵׁם־הַמֶּלֶךְ וְנַחְתּוֹם בְּטַבַּעַת הַמֶּלֶךְ אֵין לְהָשִׁיב:

8 ¹ON THAT DAY, King Achashverosh gave to Queen Esther the estate of Haman, the oppressor of the Jews, and Mordechai came before the king, for Esther had told [the king] what [relation] he was to her. ²The king then took off his ring that he had removed from Haman, and gave it to Mordechai, and Esther appointed Mordechai over Haman's estate. ³Esther then spoke again before the king and fell before his feet. She wept and entreated him to abolish the evil [decree] of Haman the Agagi, and his plan that he had devised against the Jews. ⁴The king stretched out the golden scepter to Esther, and Esther arose and stood before the king. ⁵She then said, "If it pleases the king and the king regards me favorably, and [if] the king approves of the matter and I am pleasing to him, let it be written to recall the bills [of law], the plan of Haman the son of Hamedasa, the Agagi, that he wrote to annihilate [all] the Jews who are in all the king's states. ⁶For how can I witness the misfortune that will befall my people, and how can I witness the annihilation of my kin?!" ⁷King Achashverosh then said to Queen Esther and to Mordechai the Jew, "I have indeed given Haman's estate to Esther, and him they hanged on the gallows because he acted against the Jews. ⁸So you, write in the name of the king as you see fit concerning the Jews, and seal [it] with the king's signet ring, for a document that was written in the name of the king and firmly sealed with the king's signet ring cannot be recalled."

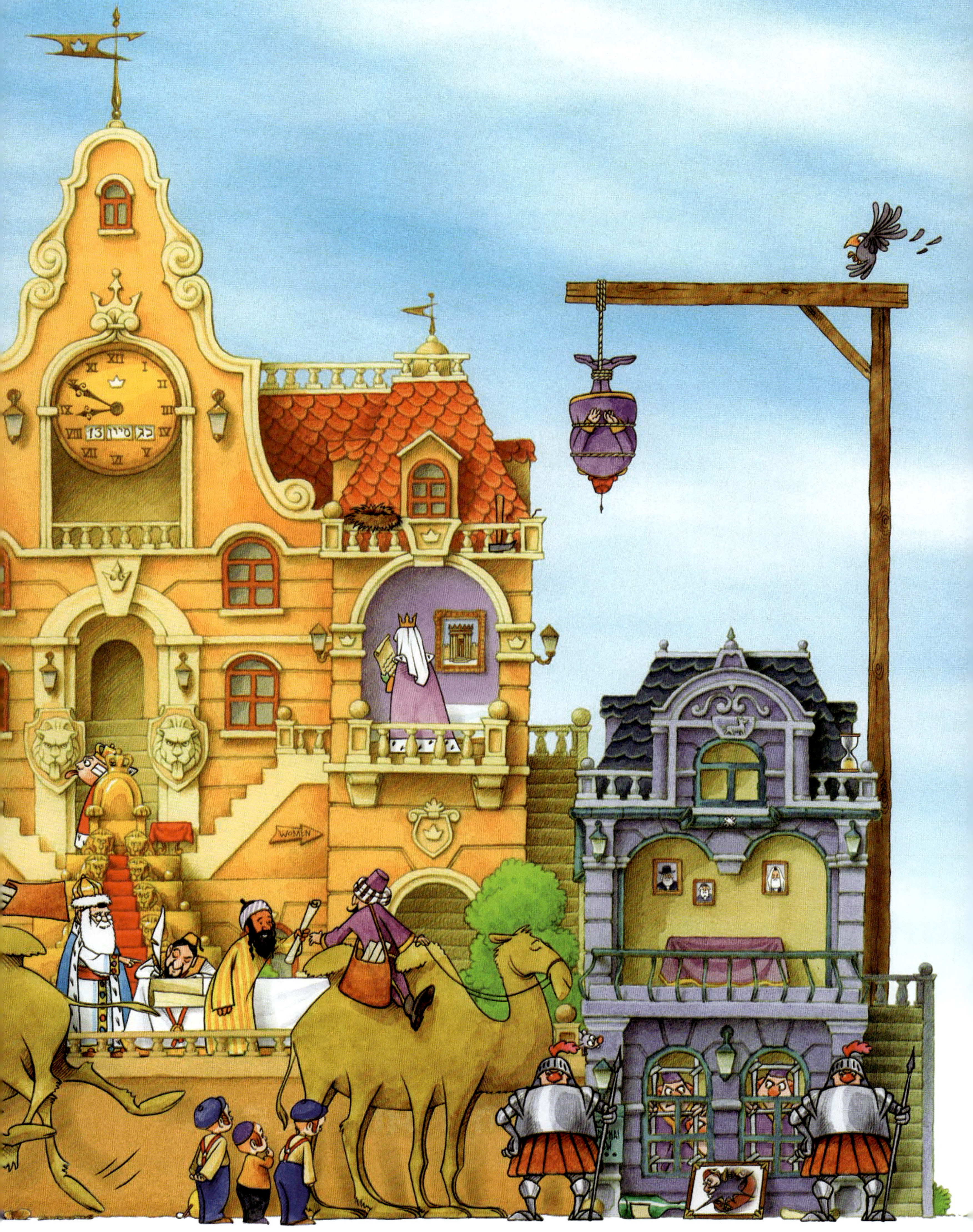

52

⁹At that time, in the third month, the month of Sivan, on the twenty-third of [the month], the king's scribes were summoned, and whatever Mordechai ordered concerning the Jews, and concerning the satraps, governors and ministers of the states that extended from Hodu to Kush—one hundred and twenty-seven states—was written down; [to] each state according to its [form of] script, and [to] each nation according to its language; and to the Jews, [as well,] according to their [form of] script and language. ¹⁰[Mordechai] had [all this] written in the name of the king, and sealed [it] with the king's signet ring. He then sent out bills [of law] with the swift horse riders [and] the riders of the king's elite express camels [and] young ponies, ¹¹[stating] that the king had allowed the Jews in every city to group together and protect their lives, [and] to destroy, kill and annihilate any army of a people or state that attacks them, [and their] children and women, and to plunder their [property as] spoil; ¹²on one day, in all the states of King Achashverosh—on the thirteenth of the twelfth month, the month of Adar. ¹³The text of the document was to become law in every state, publicized for all the nations, and for the Jews to be prepared for this day to avenge themselves of their enemies. ¹⁴The swift riders, the riders of the king's elite express camels, set out in a rush and hurry with the king's decree, and the law was published in Shushan, the capital. ¹⁵**Mordechai then came out from before the king with royal robes of aquamarine and white, a large golden crown, a fine linen cloak and a purple [wool cloak], and the city of Shushan was jubilant and joyful.** ¹⁶**For the Jews there was [then] enlightenment, joy, elation and honor.** ¹⁷And in every state and every city—wherever the king's decree reached and his law [took effect]—there was joy and elation for the Jews, [with] feasting and a holiday; and many of the common people converted to Judaism, for they were afraid of the Jews.

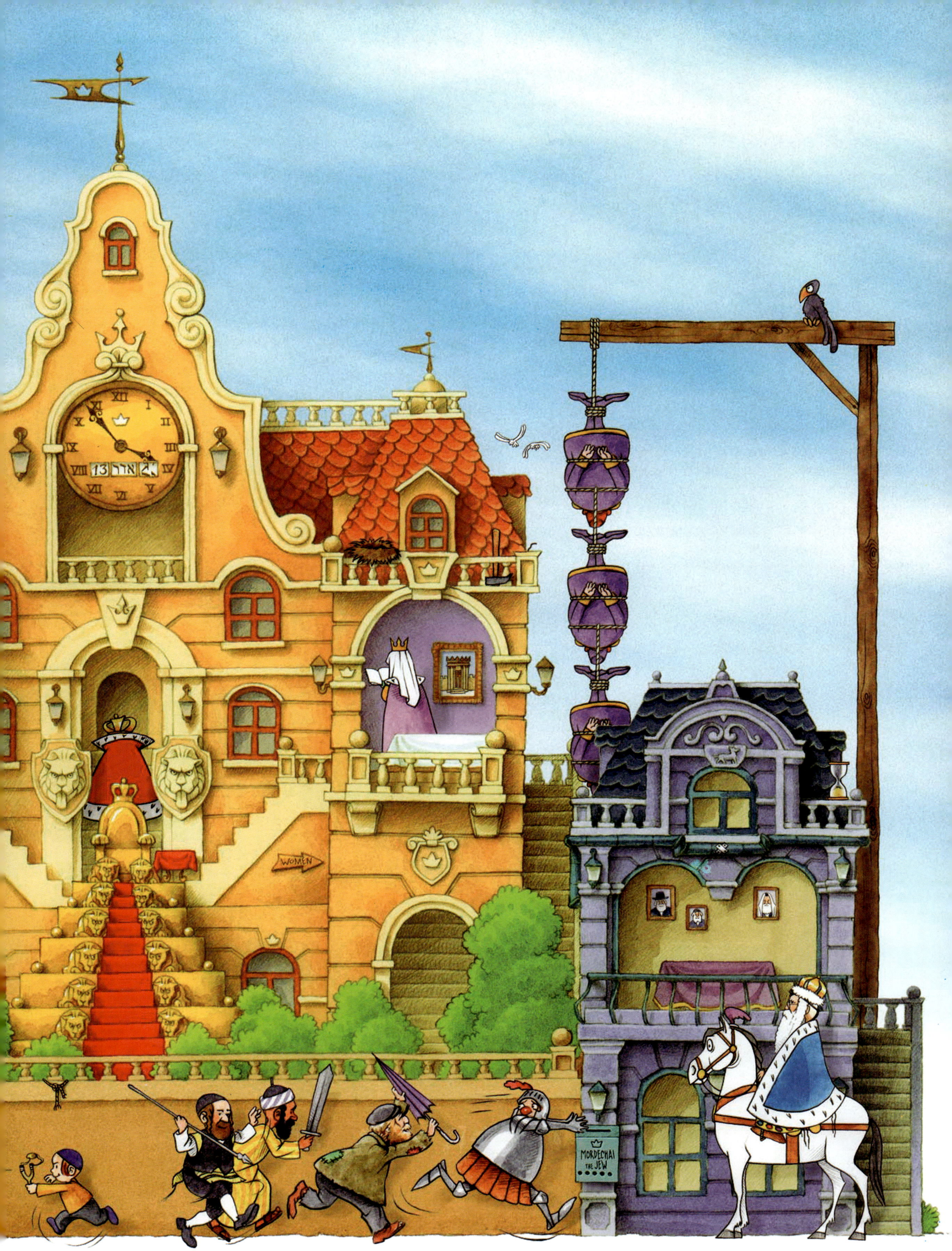

54

9 ¹ AND IN THE TWELFTH MONTH, the month of Adar, on the thirteenth day of [the month], when [the time] came for the king's decree and law to be carried out—on the day the enemies of the Jews had hoped to gain power over them, but [the situation] was reversed, that the Jews could [now] gain power over their enemies— ² the Jews grouped together in their cities, in all the states of King Achashverosh, to act against those who sought them harm, but no man [even] stood in their way, for all the nations were afraid of them. ³ And the state ministers, satraps and governors, and the administrators of the king's affairs raised the status of the Jews, since they were afraid of Mordechai. ⁴ For Mordechai was esteemed in the king's household and his fame spread throughout the states, because the [great] man, Mordechai, was steadily becoming greater. ⁵ The Jews smote their enemies with the sword and [other forms of] killing and extermination, and did as they wished to those who hated them. ⁶ And in Shushan, the capital, the Jews killed and annihilated five hundred men. ⁷ And Parshandasa and Dalfon and Aspasa, ⁸ and Porasa and Adalya and Aridasa ⁹ and Parmashta and Arisai and Aridai and Vaizasa, ¹⁰ the ten sons of Haman the son of Hamdasa, the oppressor of the Jews, they killed, but they did not lay their hands on [any of] the booty. ¹¹ On that day, the number of those killed in Shushan the capital came before the king. ¹² The king then said to Queen Esther, "In Shushan the capital the Jews killed and annihilated five hundred men and the ten sons of Haman. In the other states of the king what did they do? And what is your request and it will be granted you? And what further wish do you have and it will be done?" ¹³ Esther answered, "If it pleases the king, let tomorrow, as well, be given for the Jews in Shushan to act according to the law [that applied] today, and let them hang the ten sons of Haman on the gallows." ¹⁴ The king declared that this be done and it was made law in Shushan, and the ten sons of Haman they hanged. ¹⁵ The Jews in Shushan grouped together also on the fourteenth of the month of Adar and killed three hundred men in Shushan, but they did not lay their hands on [any of] the booty. ¹⁶ And the rest of the Jews in the [other] states of the king grouped together, protecting their lives, and were relieved of their enemies and killed seventy-five thousand of those who hated them, but they did not lay their hands on [any of] the booty.

יז בְּיוֹם שְׁלוֹשָׁה עָשָׂר לְחֹדֶשׁ אֲדָר וְנוֹחַ בְּאַרְבָּעָה עָשָׂר בּוֹ וְעָשֹׂה אֹתוֹ יוֹם מִשְׁתֶּה וְשִׂמְחָה: יח וְהַיְּהוּדִיִּים יתיר י׳ אֲשֶׁר בְּשׁוּשָׁן נִקְהֲלוּ בִּשְׁלוֹשָׁה עָשָׂר בּוֹ וּבְאַרְבָּעָה עָשָׂר בּוֹ וְנוֹחַ בַּחֲמִשָּׁה עָשָׂר בּוֹ וְעָשֹׂה אֹתוֹ יוֹם מִשְׁתֶּה וְשִׂמְחָה: יט עַל כֵּן הַיְּהוּדִים הַפְּרָזִים יתיר י׳ הַיֹּשְׁבִים בְּעָרֵי הַפְּרָזוֹת עֹשִׂים אֵת יוֹם אַרְבָּעָה עָשָׂר לְחֹדֶשׁ אֲדָר שִׂמְחָה וּמִשְׁתֶּה וְיוֹם טוֹב וּמִשְׁלֹחַ מָנוֹת אִישׁ לְרֵעֵהוּ: כ וַיִּכְתֹּב

[17] [This was] on the thirteenth of the month of Adar, and they rested on the fourteenth, making it a day of feasting and joy. [18] But the Jews in Shushan grouped together on the thirteenth and fourteenth of [the month], and rested on the fifteenth, making it a day of feasting and joy. [19] Therefore, the rural Jews who live in the open towns observe the fourteenth day of the month of Adar as [a day of] joy and feasting and a holiday, with the sending of food gifts, each to his friend. [20] Mordechai wrote down these events, and sent letters to all the Jews

מָרְדֳּכַי אֶת הַדְּבָרִים הָאֵלֶּה וַיִּשְׁלַח סְפָרִים אֶל כָּל הַיְּהוּדִים אֲשֶׁר בְּכָל מְדִינוֹת הַמֶּלֶךְ אֲחַשְׁוֵרוֹשׁ הַקְּרוֹבִים וְהָרְחוֹקִים: כא לְקַיֵּם עֲלֵיהֶם לִהְיוֹת עֹשִׂים אֵת יוֹם אַרְבָּעָה עָשָׂר לְחֹדֶשׁ אֲדָר וְאֵת יוֹם חֲמִשָּׁה עָשָׂר בּוֹ בְּכָל שָׁנָה וְשָׁנָה: כב כַּיָּמִים אֲשֶׁר נָחוּ בָהֶם הַיְּהוּדִים מֵאֹיְבֵיהֶם וְהַחֹדֶשׁ אֲשֶׁר נֶהְפַּךְ לָהֶם מִיָּגוֹן לְשִׂמְחָה וּמֵאֵבֶל לְיוֹם טוֹב לַעֲשׂוֹת אוֹתָם יְמֵי מִשְׁתֶּה וְשִׂמְחָה וּמִשְׁלֹחַ מָנוֹת אִישׁ לְרֵעֵהוּ וּמַתָּנוֹת לָאֶבְיֹנִים: כג וְקִבֵּל הַיְּהוּדִים אֵת אֲשֶׁר הֵחֵלּוּ לַעֲשׂוֹת וְאֵת אֲשֶׁר כָּתַב מָרְדֳּכַי אֲלֵיהֶם: כד כִּי הָמָן בֶּן הַמְּדָתָא הָאֲגָגִי צֹרֵר כָּל הַיְּהוּדִים חָשַׁב עַל הַיְּהוּדִים לְאַבְּדָם וְהִפִּל פּוּר הוּא הַגּוֹרָל לְהֻמָּם וּלְאַבְּדָם: כה וּבְבֹאָהּ לִפְנֵי הַמֶּלֶךְ אָמַר עִם הַסֵּפֶר יָשׁוּב מַחֲשַׁבְתּוֹ הָרָעָה אֲשֶׁר חָשַׁב עַל הַיְּהוּדִים עַל רֹאשׁוֹ וְתָלוּ אֹתוֹ וְאֶת בָּנָיו עַל הָעֵץ: כו עַל כֵּן קָרְאוּ לַיָּמִים הָאֵלֶּה פוּרִים עַל שֵׁם הַפּוּר עַל כֵּן עַל כָּל דִּבְרֵי הָאִגֶּרֶת הַזֹּאת וּמָה רָאוּ עַל כָּכָה וּמָה הִגִּיעַ אֲלֵיהֶם: כז קִיְּמוּ וְקִבְּלוּ ק׳ הַיְּהוּדִים עֲלֵיהֶם וְעַל זַרְעָם וְעַל כָּל הַנִּלְוִים עֲלֵיהֶם וְלֹא יַעֲבוֹר לִהְיוֹת עֹשִׂים אֵת שְׁנֵי הַיָּמִים הָאֵלֶּה כִּכְתָבָם וְכִזְמַנָּם בְּכָל שָׁנָה וְשָׁנָה: כח וְהַיָּמִים הָאֵלֶּה נִזְכָּרִים וְנַעֲשִׂים בְּכָל דּוֹר וָדוֹר מִשְׁפָּחָה וּמִשְׁפָּחָה מְדִינָה וּמְדִינָה וְעִיר וָעִיר וִימֵי הַפּוּרִים הָאֵלֶּה לֹא יַעַבְרוּ מִתּוֹךְ הַיְּהוּדִים וְזִכְרָם לֹא יָסוּף מִזַּרְעָם: כט וַתִּכְתֹּב אֶסְתֵּר הַמַּלְכָּה בַת אֲבִיחַיִל וּמָרְדֳּכַי הַיְּהוּדִי אֶת כָּל תֹּקֶף לְקַיֵּם אֵת אִגֶּרֶת הַפֻּרִים הַזֹּאת הַשֵּׁנִית: ל וַיִּשְׁלַח סְפָרִים אֶל כָּל הַיְּהוּדִים אֶל שֶׁבַע וְעֶשְׂרִים וּמֵאָה מְדִינָה מַלְכוּת אֲחַשְׁוֵרוֹשׁ דִּבְרֵי שָׁלוֹם וֶאֱמֶת: לא לְקַיֵּם אֵת יְמֵי הַפֻּרִים הָאֵלֶּה בִּזְמַנֵּיהֶם כַּאֲשֶׁר קִיַּם עֲלֵיהֶם מָרְדֳּכַי הַיְּהוּדִי וְאֶסְתֵּר הַמַּלְכָּה וְכַאֲשֶׁר קִיְּמוּ עַל נַפְשָׁם וְעַל זַרְעָם דִּבְרֵי הַצֹּמוֹת וְזַעֲקָתָם: לב וּמַאֲמַר אֶסְתֵּר קִיַּם דִּבְרֵי הַפֻּרִים הָאֵלֶּה וְנִכְתָּב בַּסֵּפֶר:

in all the states of King Achashverosh, those near and far, [21] [for them] to take upon themselves to observe each year the fourteenth day of the month of Adar and the fifteenth, [22] like the days on which the Jews rested from [fighting] their enemies, and [in] the month that was transformed for them from misery to joy, and from mourning to a holiday; [for the Jews] to observe them as days of feasting and joy, with the sending of food gifts, each to his friend, and donations to the needy. [23] The Jews [unanimously] accepted upon themselves that which they had begun to observe, and [those laws] which Mordechai had written for them [to keep]. [24] For Haman the son of Hamedasa, the Agagi, the oppressor of all the Jews, devised [a plan] against the Jews to annihilate them, and cast Pur, which is the lot, to throw them into confusion and to annihilate them. [25] But when [Esther] came before the king [and entreated him, the king] said, with [his words being written down as] bills of law, [that Haman's] evil plan which he devised against the Jews be reversed [to fall] upon his [own] head, and they hanged him and his sons on the gallows. [26] Therefore, they called these days Purim on account of the Pur. [To publicize] this, all the words of this letter [were written], and [to tell] what prompted [these people to act] this way, and what [subsequently] happened to them. [27] The Jews took and accepted upon themselves and their descendants, and upon all those who join them — and it must not be transgressed — to observe these two days; [and that the scroll be written] according to its [prescribed form of] script; and [that the days be observed] at their [proper] time each year; [28] and [that] these days [be] commemorated and observed in every generation, every family, every state and every city; and [that] these days of Purim shall not disappear from among the Jews, and their commemoration shall not cease from [among] their descendants. [29] Queen Esther, the daughter of Avichayil, with Mordechai the Jew, wrote down the magnitude of all [the miracles], so as to establish this second letter of Purim. [30] [Mordechai] then sent letters to all the Jews — to the hundred and twenty-seven states, the kingdom of Achashverosh — [with] words of peace and truth, [31] in order to establish these days of Purim at their [prescribed] times, just as Mordechai the Jew and Queen Esther had instituted for them, and just as they had taken upon themselves and their descendants, [as well as] the fasts and their prayers. [32] And [through] Esther's petition, these words of [the letter of] Purim were established and written in the book [of Holy Writings].

י א וַיָּשֶׂם הַמֶּלֶךְ אֲחַשְׁרֵשׁ אֲחַשְׁוֵרוֹשׁ ק׳ מַס עַל הָאָרֶץ וְאִיֵּי הַיָּם: ב וְכָל מַעֲשֵׂה תָקְפּוֹ וּגְבוּרָתוֹ וּפָרָשַׁת גְּדֻלַּת מָרְדֳּכַי אֲשֶׁר גִּדְּלוֹ הַמֶּלֶךְ הֲלוֹא הֵם כְּתוּבִים עַל סֵפֶר דִּבְרֵי הַיָּמִים לְמַלְכֵי מָדַי וּפָרָס: ג כִּי מָרְדֳּכַי הַיְּהוּדִי מִשְׁנֶה לַמֶּלֶךְ אֲחַשְׁוֵרוֹשׁ וְגָדוֹל לַיְּהוּדִים וְרָצוּי לְרֹב אֶחָיו דֹּרֵשׁ טוֹב לְעַמּוֹ וְדֹבֵר שָׁלוֹם לְכָל זַרְעוֹ:

10 [1] KING ACHASHVEROSH then imposed a tax, [both] on the mainland and the sea islands. [2] And the entire account of his power and might, and the details of Mordechai's greatness [to which] the king promoted him, are indeed written in the book of chronicles of the kings of Madai and Paras. [3] **For Mordechai the Jew was King Achashverosh's viceroy, the leader of the Jews, and accepted by most of his brethren, promoting his people's welfare and preaching peace for all their descendants.**

שׁוֹשַׁנַּת יַעֲקֹב צָהֲלָה וְשָׂמֵחָה בִּרְאוֹתָם יַחַד תְּכֵלֶת מָרְדְּכָי, תְּשׁוּעָתָם הָיִיתָ לָנֶצַח וְתִקְוָתָם בְּכָל דּוֹר וָדוֹר, לְהוֹדִיעַ שֶׁכָּל קוֶֹיךָ לֹא יֵבֹשׁוּ, וְלֹא יִכָּלְמוּ לָנֶצַח כָּל הַחוֹסִים בָּךְ. אָרוּר הָמָן אֲשֶׁר בִּקֵּשׁ לְאַבְּדִי, בָּרוּךְ מָרְדְּכַי הַיְּהוּדִי, אֲרוּרָה זֶרֶשׁ אֵשֶׁת מַפְחִידִי, בְּרוּכָה אֶסְתֵּר בַּעֲדִי, וְגַם חַרְבוֹנָה זָכוּר לַטּוֹב.

The Rose of Ya'akov [the Jewish people] was jubilant and joyful when they jointly beheld the aquamarine [robe] of Mordechai. You have always been their salvation, and their hope in every generation, to make known that all who hope in You will not be ashamed, nor will those who take refuge in You ever be disgraced. Cursed is Haman who sought to annihilate me; blessed is Mordechai the Jew. Cursed is Zeresh, the wife of him who terrified me; blessed is Esther who shielded me. And Charvonah, too, is remembered

59

Source material
from Midrash and Chazal

Pages 6-7

"On his royal throne." Rabbi Kohen in the name of Rabbi Azaryah observed: The word *malchuso* (his royal) could be read as *melachto* (his handiwork). This teaches us that when Achashverosh came to sit on Shelomo's throne, his advisers did not let him. They cautioned him that any king who was not a universal ruler could not sit on it. So he went and made a replica of it for himself. The text therefore means, "On a throne of his own making." *Esther Rabbah 1:12.*

Rabbi Levi said: "He showed them the garments of the High Priest. They are spoken of here as 'The **glory** of his greatness,' and referred to in the Torah (*Shemos 28:2*): 'You shall make sacred garments for your brother, Aharon, for [his] honor and **glory**.' Just as the 'glory' used there refers to the garments of the High Priest, so does the term 'glory' used here refer to the garments of the High Priest." *Esther Rabbah 2:1.*

When he brought out his own vessels and [compared them to] the vessels of the Temple, [he found] the Temple vessels more pleasing than his own. *Esther Rabbah 2:11.*

Just as his [displayed] the garments of the High Priest, so did hers [display] the garments of the High Priest. *Esther Rabbah 3:9.*

He made a feast for them and ordered all of them to come and eat and drink and do as they please. As it is written, "To carry out the [individual] wishes of each person." When Mordechai realized this, he arose and proclaimed to [the Jews] and said, "Do not go to eat at the banquet of Achashverosh. For he has only invited you to lay a trap for you, to create an opportunity for the Attribute of Justice to accuse you before the Holy Blessed One." *Esther Rabbah 7:14.*

The seven-day banquet in Shushan began during the Ten Days of Repentance and was to run through Yom Kippur. That is why Mordechai warned the Jews against taking part in that banquet. *Yalkut Me'am Lo'ez 1:5 in the name of the Ya'aros Devash.*

"And [any amount of] drink was in order." What is meant by "in order"? Said Rav Chanan in the name of Rabbi Meir, "In order according to the Torah [i.e., kosher]." *Megillah 12a.*

To carry out the wishes of each Jewish person, and the wishes of each non-Jewish person. *Targum Rishon 1:8.*

Queen Vashti was the daughter of Evil-Merodach, and the granddaughter of Nevuchadnetzar king of Bavel. *Targum Sheini 1:12.*

The nation of Yisrael is likened to a dove, as it is written, "[Like] wings of the dove – covered with silver." *Sanhedrin 95a*.

"Haman's Ears" - because his ears were pulled (he was shamed). *Shevilei ha-Minhag*, quoting *Sefer Purim and the Month of Adar*.

Pages 8-9

"On the seventh day." Rabbi Yehoshu'a ben Levi says that it was the Sabbath. (How Erev Yom Kippur could fall on the Sabbath needs further investigation.) *Esther Rabbah 3:11*.

They did not heed the words of Mordechai, and they all went to the banquet hall. *Esther Rabbah 7:14*.

Rav Eivo said: "[When Yisrael eat and drink and make merry,] they bless and praise and exalt the Holy Blessed One. When the gentiles eat and drink, they immerse themselves in indecent talk. One claimed that Median women were the most beautiful, while another claimed that Persian women were the most beautiful." *Esther Rabbah 3:13*.

"But Queen Vashti refused to come." [This was because the angel] Gavriel came and made her a tail. *Megillah 12b*.

There is a universal custom that on Purim young men make an effigy of Haman and string it up. *Minhag Yisrael Torah 690:3*.

Pages 10-11

"And [so] the king was extremely enraged and his fury burned within him." Said Rabbi Yochanan: "At that moment, the Holy Blessed One ordered the angel in charge of anger, 'Go down and blow a blast into his belly. Blow the embers and throw sulfur into his stove!'" *Esther Rabbah 3:15*.

Another said it was because he (Memuchan) had a daughter, and he sought to have her marry into royalty. *Esther Rabbah 4:6*.

Pages 12-13

He (Achashverosh) became angry and ordered that the seven ministers be hanged. *Targum Sheini 2:1.*

"... and your brother becomes poor with him." This refers to Yisrael, who were poor and needy. *Esther Rabbah 10:13.*

"... I will utterly wipe out [any] trace [or, memory - *zecher*] of Amalek." This refers to Haman, who is called the man (*zachar*) of Amalek. *Esther Rabbah 10:13.*

Haman is compared to a wolf. *Esther Rabbah 10:13.*

Pages 14-15

Until he crowned Esther, he (Achashverosh) kept an [engraved] image of Vashti. *Esther Rabbah 6:11.*

Know that Haman slipped his daughter in among the other young girls, hoping the king would choose her to replace Vashti. But Hashem made her smell bad. *Yalkut Me'am Lo'ez 2:4.*

They called her Esther (*hidden*), because she was secluded in Mordechai's home. *Targum Rishon 2:7.*

Some have the custom on Purim of writing the names of Amalek and Haman, and later erasing them with liquor. *Sefer ha-Toda'ah 2:45.*

62

Pages 16-17

Said Rabbi Yochanan: "Bigsan and Teresh were two Tarseans, and they conversed in the Tarsean language. They said, '…Come, let us put poison in [the king's] cup so that he will die.' But they did not know that Mordechai was a member of the Sanhedrin, and that he understood seventy languages." *Megillah 13b.*

"Let us put snake venom in the golden cup from which he drinks, so that when he wants to drink he will die." *Yalkut Me'am Lo'ez 2:21.*

"We can't do that, because when I am on duty I must bring the king water, while your job is to give him other sweetened drinks. To carry out the plot we must work the same shift." *ibid.*

Rabbi Yehoshu'a ben Korcha said: "Esther was greenish, but endowed with much grace." *Megillah 13a.*

Hegai sent her home in disgrace. *Yalkut Me'am Lo'ez 2:4.*

Esther was taken by force and brought to the king's palace. *Targum Rishon 2:8.*

Once he married Esther, well-bred and of noble bearing, he gave the order to remove Vashti's image and put up Esther's instead. This is what is meant by, "And he made her queen instead of Vashti." *Esther Rabbah 6:11.*

Pages 18-19

After Esther revealed the plot to Achashverosh, he took the cup and gave it to one of his animals (it is common for kings to raise animals). The animal's stomach burst and it died. *Yalkut Me'am Lo'ez 2:21.*

Pages 20-21

What did Haman do? He made for himself an image embroidered on his clothing and on his heart. Hence, everyone who bowed down to Haman would [also] be bowing to an idol. *Esther Rabbah 7:8*.

Mordechai would show [Haman] his foot on which was written that [Haman] was his slave.(See notes on page 4.) So Haman prepared himself for hanging, since he himself had written that if he would deny that he had sold himself to Mordechai, he would be hanged. That is why Mordechai was not worried at all; he was certain that Haman would be hanged. *Yalkut Me'am Lo'ez 3:2*.

Achashverosh was a foolish king. *Megillah 12a*.

"He is [the same] Achashverosh" – a foolish king. *Targum Sheini 1:1*.

"He made his position higher." He made himself a platform above his [regular] platform, [to raise himself] above all the ministers. *Yalkut Shim'oni 3*.

Pages 22-23

What was Mordechai's response to the one who asked him, "Why do you disobey the king's command?" Rabbi Levi said [that Mordechai answered]: "Moshe, our teacher, warned us in the Torah (*Devarim 27*), 'Cursed is the man who makes a crafted statue or metal image.' And this evil one makes himself into an idol! And the prophet Yeshayah warned us (*Yeshayah 2:22*), 'Withdraw from man who has breath in his nostrils, for with what is he deemed worthy?' Not only that, but I am an aristocrat of the Holy Blessed One. For all of the tribes were born outside of the land [of Yisrael], except for my ancestor [Binyamin], who was born in the land of Yisrael." *Esther Rabbah 7:8*.

He cast dice, which have dots on all sides, as is well-known. On opposite sides are four dots and three dots. The same with six and one. That evil man played with three dice. On one of them he got one dot, and on the other two, three dots each. He was happy that they spelled out Agag (one [Aleph], three [Gimmel], and three [Gimmel] spell out AGaG). *Yalkut Me'am Lo'ez 3:7*.

64

"Then Charvonah said…" Said Rabbi El'azar: "Charvonah also was a wicked man and implicated in that plot." *Megillah 16a*.

Pages 24-25

"But Mordechai knew." Eliyahu informed him. *Targum Sheini 4:1*.

When he turned over the dice to see what was on their underside, four dots showed up on two of them, because opposite three dots there appear four. Six dots were on the bottom of third die. Four (Dalet), six (Vav), and four (Dalet) spell out DaViD (David), whose Gematria totals fourteen. Hence he was happy, for Agag came up on top, while David was on the bottom. *Yalkut Me'am Lo'ez 3:7*.

We may deduce that also Achashverosh had wanted to annihilate them. *Rashi, Megillah 14a*.

Pages 26-27

Incomparable peace unto you! Let it be known to you that there is a man among us who is not from our land, but he is of royal descent and of the descendants of Amalek. He is one of the great ones of our generation, and Haman is his name. He made one small, simple request of one nation among us, the most despised of all nations. They are arrogant. They wish us evil, and they constantly curse the king. How do they curse us? [They say (*Tehillim 10:16*),] "The Eternal is king forevermore; the nations have perished from His land." They also say (*ibid. 149:7*), "… to execute vengeance upon the nations, chastisements upon the peoples," and they reject whoever benefited them.

See, for example, what they did to that poor Par'oh. When they came down to Mitzrayim, he accepted them cheerfully, settled them in the best part of the land, nourished them in the years of hunger, and fed them all the good things of the land. [Par'oh] had to build palaces, and had them participate in building them, but he could not control them. Not only that, but they came to him with a pretense and told him (*Shemos 5:3*), "Let us go on a three-day journey and sacrifice to our God. After that, we will return. Please lend us vessels of silver and gold, and clothing." So the people loaned them their silver and gold and all their good clothing. Then every one [of the Jews] loaded up so many of their donkeys beyond number, until they emptied Mitzrayim, as it is written (*ibid. 12:36*), "They [thus] drained the Mitzrim [of their wealth]." Then they ran away. When Par'oh heard that they were running away, he went after them to retrieve his money. What did he do to them? There was a man with them whose name was Moshe, the son of Amram. With his sorcery, he took a stick, uttered incantations over it, and struck the sea until it became dry. Then they all entered onto the dry land in the midst of the sea, and they all crossed over it. I do not know how they crossed over it and how the waters dried up. When Par'oh saw that, he entered after them to retrieve his money. I do not know how they propelled him into the midst of the sea, and drowned him and all his army. They did not remember the good he did for them. See how ungrateful they are!

Furthermore [said Haman], what did they do to my forefather Amalek when he came upon them in battle? As it is written (*ibid. 17:8*), "Amalek then came and fought with Yisrael at Refidim." From where was Amalek coming? Rabbi Kruspedai said in the name of Rabbi Yochanan: He came from meeting with the evil Bil'am. [Amalek] had come to get advice from him, and told him, "I know you are someone who provides counsel, and that you also harbor malevolent thoughts [toward Yisrael]. Anyone who follows your advice does not fail." He [further] said to [Bil'am], "See what these people did to Mitzrayim, who did so much good for them. If they did this to Mitzrayim, who did so many good things for them, imagine what they would do to other nations! What do you advise me to do?" Bil'am advised him, "Go make war with them. If you do not make war with them, you will not be able to overcome them, because they depend on the merit of their forefather Avraham. You, too, who are a descendant of Avraham, rely on Avraham's merit." So he immediately attacked them. What did their leader Moshe do? He had a disciple named Yehoshu'a bin Nun, who was exceedingly cruel and merciless. This Moshe said to him (*ibid. 17:9*), "Choose men for us, and go out and fight against Amalek." I do not know whether those people he chose were sorcerers or warriors. What did this Moshe do? He took a staff in his hand, but I do not know what he did with it. When [Yehoshu'a] came upon them, I do not know what incantation [Moshe] pronounced upon them, but their hands weakened and they fell before them, as it is written (*ibid. 17:13*), "Yehoshu'a weakened Amalek and his people by the sword."

They attacked Sichon and Og, the great warriors of our land, whom no one could challenge. How [Yisrael] killed them, I do not know. The same with the kings of Midyan. Furthermore, what did [Yehoshu'a,] the disciple of this man Moshe, do? He brought Yisrael into the land of Kena'an. It was not enough that he took away their land, but he also killed thirty-one of their kings and divided their land among Yisrael. He took no pity on them, and those whom he did not want to kill became servants to him. Sisera and his multitude attacked them. I do not know what they did to the Kishon Brook that swept them up, washed them away and threw them into the great sea, as it is written (*Shofetim 5:21*), "Kishon Brook swept them up."

They had their first king, whose name was Sha'ul. He went to battle in the land of my forefather Amalek and killed one hundred thousand of their horsemen in a single day. He took pity on neither man, woman, child nor suckling (see *Shemuel I 15:1-8*). I do not know why he killed them.

Moreover, what did he do to my grandfather Agag, upon whom they first took pity? In the end, a man of theirs came whose name was Shemuel, cut him up, and gave his flesh as food to the birds of the skies, as it is written (*ibid. 15:33*), "Shemuel then cut Agag into quarters." I do not know why he killed him by such an unusual death, as you have just heard. After that, they had a king named David, the son of Yishai, who destroyed and annihilated all the kingdoms. He took no pity on them, as it is written (*ibid. 27:11*), "David would leave alive neither man nor woman." After him, his son Shelomo arose, built a house for Yisrael, and called it the Temple. I do not know what they had inside it. Whenever they went to battle, they would enter it and perform sorcery. When they came out and went to war, they would kill and destroy the world. Due to the excessive good that they enjoyed, they rebelled against their God. In addition, that God of theirs became old. Nevuchadnetzar then came and burned that house of theirs, exiled them from their soil and brought them among us.

Yet, they have not changed their ugly ways. Even though they are exiled among us, they ridicule us and the faith of our gods. Now, we have all agreed to a single policy, and we have cast lots to annihilate them from the world. At which time could we likely finish them off? The lottery fell upon them for the thirteenth day of the month of Adar. Now, when these letters reach you, be ready for that day, to destroy and kill all the Jews among us, young and old, children and women, in a single day, and let none of them remain as a survivor or refugee. *Esther Rabbah 7:13*.

Pages 28-29

"Esther said to send this response to Mordechai." She said to him, "Go [and] congregate all the Jews located in Shushan, and [proclaim a] fast on my behalf, that you will not eat or drink for three days, night and day." These were 13-15 Nissan. [Mordechai] sent word to her that these days include the first day of Pesach. She responded to him, "Elder of Yisrael! What is Pesach for [if there be no more Yisrael]? Some say that they fasted on the 14th, 15th and 16th (*Rashi*). Immediately, Mordechai understood and agreed to her words, since if Yisrael would be destroyed, so would the mitzvos. To paraphrase the Sages: "Better to desecrate one Pesach in order to observe future Pesachs." *Esther Rabbah 8:7*.

At that moment, Esther was very much afraid because of the evil that had emerged against Yisrael. She removed her royal garb and her [crown of] glory, and she donned sackcloth. She uncovered the hair of her head and filled it with dust and ashes, and tormented herself with fasting. And she fell on her face before Hashem and prayed. *Esther Rabbah 8:7.*

Then they chose from the assembly twelve thousand young priests, and gave them to hold a shofar in their right hand and a Torah in their left, and they cried out and exclaimed. *Targum Sheini 4:16.*

Pages 30-31

[Mordechai] asked one of them, "Recite to me the verse [you learned today]." He replied (*Mishlei 3:25*), "Do not be afraid of sudden terror, or of the darkness of the wicked when it will come." *Esther Rabbah 7:17.*

Rabbi Yochanan said: "Three ministering angels were appointed to help her at that moment; one to make her head erect, a second to endow her with charm, and a third to stretch the golden scepter." How much was it stretched? Rabbi Yirmeyah said, "It was two cubits long and he made it twelve." Some say sixteen, and others say twenty-four. In a *baraisa* it was stated, sixty. *Megillah 15b.*

Pages 32-33

The second child responded by saying, "This is the last verse I learned in school today (*Yeshayah 8:10*): 'Take counsel and it will be foiled; speak a word and it will not succeed, for God is with us.'" *Esther Rabbah 7:17.*

Pages 34-35

The third boy quoted the verse (*Yeshayah 46:4*): "Even until your seniority I remain unchanged, and even until your ripe old age, I will carry you; I made you and I will bear you, I will carry you and rescue you." *Esther Rabbah 7:17*.

Sleep eluded King Achashverosh, because he dreamt that Haman was wielding a sword to kill him. *Esther Rabbah 10:1*.

Pages 36-37

Rabbi Chama bar Guryon said, "No one slept that night." *Yalkut Shim'oni 6:1*.

Esther was busy preparing Haman's feast. *ibid*.

Mordechai was absorbed in his sackcloth and fasting. *ibid*.

Haman was preoccupied with his gallows. *ibid*.

He measured himself against it to show his servants how to hang Mordechai on it. A heavenly voice remarked, "The hanging tree fits you perfectly. It has been ready for you since the six days of Creation." *Esther Rabbah 9:2*.

Haman's son, Shimshi the scribe, came across what Mordechai had told about Bigsan and Teresh, but he turned the pages, not wanting to read it to the king. The Master of the Universe, however, did want it, and the pages turned by themselves, and what was written on those pages was read out before the king. *Targum Sheini 6:1*.

Pages 38-39

After he prepared the gallows, he went to Mordechai and found him sitting in the house of study. The young children were sitting before him dressed in sackcloth, learning Torah, sobbing and weeping. [Haman] counted them and found twenty-two thousand young children there. He threw them in iron chains, appointed guards over them and said, "Tomorrow I will kill these little children first, and afterward I will hang Mordechai." *Esther Rabbah 9:4.*

Their mothers would bring them bread and water and say to them, "Our children! Eat and drink before you die tomorrow; do not die of starvation." Immediately, they placed their hands on their books and swore, "By the life of Mordechai, our teacher, we will neither eat nor drink, but perish while fasting!" *ibid.*

They all wept loudly until their cries rose up to the heavens. The Holy Blessed One heard their crying after the second hour of the night. *ibid.*

Pages 40-41

"Haman took the robes and the horse." He went to Mordechai, and when they told Mordechai that [Haman] had come, he became extremely frightened. He was sitting with his disciples in front of him. He said to them, "My sons! Run and get away from here, so that you will not suffer because of me, for the evil Haman has come to kill me." They replied, "If you die, we will die with you." He said to them, "Then let us pray together and depart while praying." *Esther Rabbah 10:4.*

They sat down and immersed themselves in studying the laws of the Omer, for it was the sixteenth of Nissan, and during the Temple era, they would offer the Omer on that day. *ibid.*

Haman approached them and asked what they were studying. They answered him, "The commandment concerning the Omer." So it is written (*Vayikra 2:14*), "When you bring a meal-offering of the first-ripening grain…" [In Bavel, the Sages] said, "They showed him the laws of *kemitzah*, and the small amount that they would take out of the Omer." [Haman] asked them, "What is this Omer, gold or silver?" They replied, "It is neither gold nor silver nor wheat, but barley." He asked, "How much is it worth, ten *kanterin*?" They told him, "Ten *maneh*, at the most." Said he to them, "Get up, for your ten *maneh* have triumphed over my ten thousand *kikar* of silver." *Esther Rabbah 10:4.*

69

When Mordechai finished praying, Haman said to him, "Put on the king's clothing." He replied, "Why are you degrading the monarchy? Does a person put on royal garb without bathing?!" Haman went looking for a bathhouse attendant, but could not find one. What did he do? He girded his loins, went in and bathed him. *ibid.*

When [Mordechai] came out, [Haman] said to him, "Take this crown and put it on." He replied, "Why are you disgracing the monarchy? Does a person don the royal crown with unshorn hair?!" [Haman] went looking for a barber, but could not find one. What did he do? He went home and brought scissors, sat down and gave [Mordechai] a haircut. [Haman] started to groan, and [Mordechai] asked him, "Why are you groaning?" He answered, "Woe is my father, for I have gone from being a chief minister, to being a bathhouse attendant and a barber!" [Mordechai] replied, "That is why I asked you. Don't I know that your father was a bathhouse attendant and a barber in the village of Carianus, whose hair-cutting equipment you have now found?" *ibid.*

Said [Haman], "Get up and ride on this horse." [Mordechai] replied, "I am too weak, for I am old." [Haman] asked him, "And I, am I not old?" Said [Mordechai], "But didn't you bring this on yourself?" [Haman] said to him, "Get up, and I will lower my back for you. Step on me and go up and ride. This will fulfill for you that which is stated (*Devarim 33:29*): "... and you will tread upon their exalted ones." *Esther Rabbah 10:4.*

His daughter saw him from the roof. She thought that the rider was her father and that the one walking before him was Mordechai. So she took the chamber-pot and emptied it on her father's head. *Megillah 16a.*

Before he rode on the royal mount, she sent him from the palace twenty-seven thousand young men, each bearing a golden goblet in his right hand and a golden pitcher in his left. They sang and marched before Mordechai, the righteous one, shouting, "This is what is done to the man whom the king wishes to honor!" *Targum Sheini 6:11.*

While riding, he began praising the Holy Blessed One (*Tehillim 30:2-4*): "I will exalt You, O Eternal, for You have lifted me up, and have not let my enemies rejoice over me. O Eternal, my God, I pleaded unto You and You restored me. O Eternal, You raised my soul from *She'ol*; You saved me from descending into the pit." *Esther Rabbah 10:5.*

His disciples said (*Tehillim 30:5, 6*): "Sing to the Eternal, you, His devoted ones, and give thanks at the mention of His holy [Name]. For His anger is momentary, His favor is for a lifetime; in the evening one lies down weeping, but in the morning there is joyous singing." *Esther Rabbah 10:5.*

The wicked one (Haman) said (*Tehillim. 30:7,8*): "And as for me, I used to think in my tranquility that I would never stumble. O Eternal, through Your favor You bolstered me like a mighty mountain; when You hid Your face, I became terrified." *Esther Rabbah 10:5.*

And Esther said (*Tehillim 30:9, 10*): "Unto You, Eternal, do I cry out, and to my Lord do I plead. What gain is there in my death, in my going down into the bottomless pit? Can dust acknowledge You, can it proclaim Your truth?" *Esther Rabbah 10:5*.

Pages 42-43

"Mordechai then returned to the king's gate." Said Rav Sheshes: "He returned to his sackcloth and fasting." *Megillah 16a*.

[Haman] looked up at her and when she saw that it was her father, she jumped from the roof to the ground and killed herself. Hence it is written (*Esther 6:12*), "... while Haman hurried to his house, in mourning and his head covered." He was mourning for his daughter, and his head was covered [in dirt] because of what had happened to him. *Megillah 16a*.

Pages 44-45

"Esther replied, 'An oppressor and enemy, this evil Haman!'" Rabbi El'azar said: "This informs us that she was pointing to Achashverosh, and an angel came and pushed her hand so it would point toward Haman." *Megillah 16a*.

Pages 46-47

The king looked up and saw ten angels, who looked like Haman's sons, chopping down the trees of the inner garden. *Targum Rishon 7:7*.

The king then got up from the wine feast in a rage and went out to the inner garden to see who it was. *ibid*.

71

Pages 48-49

What did Eliyahu do, that he is remembered for the good (*zachur la-tov*)? He made himself look like Charvonah and said to [Achashverosh]: "My master, O King, there is also the gallows which Haman made for Mordechai…." As Rabbi Pinchas said: "One must say, 'As for Charvonah, he is remembered for the good (*zachur la-tov*).' Charvonah merits the same mention as Eliyahu, for they are one and the same." *Esther Rabbah 10:9*.

Pages 50-51

And young men wearing crowns, and priests holding trumpets, proclaimed: "Anyone who does not come to wish Mordechai and the Jews well will be hacked to pieces, and his house will be demolished." *Targum Rishon 8:15*.

And the ten sons of Haman marched with arms raised before Mordechai, the righteous, saying: "Who is He Who rewards the Jews and punishes the wicked? Look at our foolish father, Haman, who relied on his wealth and honor, yet the humble Mordechai crushed him with his fasting and prayer." *ibid*.

The king presented everything that Haman owned to Queen Esther, and Esther transferred it to Mordechai. *Esther Rabbah 10:9*.

The righteous Esther watched from the window, for it is improper for a queen to walk in the street with common people. Mordechai turned his gaze toward her and said (*Tehillim 124:6*), "The Eternal is a source of blessing, Who has not offered us as prey for their teeth." Esther answered him (*Tehillim 124:8*), "Our help is in the Name of the Eternal, Maker of heaven and earth." *Targum Rishon 8:15*.

"Binyamin is [like] a wolf that mauls." *Bereshis 49:27*.

Pages 52-53

In order that no one doubt the authenticity of Mordechai's letters, he waited for the first couriers to return from the faraway places so that they themselves could deliver the new letters. *Yalkut Me'am Lo'ez 8:9*.

Pages 54-55

"... and many of the common people converted to Judaism." Mordechai and Esther's converts were not true converts. *Yevamos 24b, Rashi.*

Pages 56-57

One must read the Megillah at night and again in the daytime. *Shulchan Aruch O.Ch. 687:1.*

One must give donations to at least two needy people. *Shulchan Aruch O.Ch. 694:1.*

One must drink on Purim until he cannot tell the difference between "Cursed be Haman" and "Blessed be Mordechai." *Shulchan Aruch O.Ch. 695:2.*

One must send a friend two gifts of meat or of other foods, as it is written (*Esther 9:22*), "And the sending of food **gifts**, each to his **friend**"– two gifts to one friend. *Shulchan Aruch O.Ch. 695:4.*

Pages 58-59

It was also customary to put on plays based on the events of Purim, where the actors wore various masks. *Otzar Dinim u-Minhagim.*

Even on Purim, merriment is permitted only in commemoration of Achashverosh. *Mishnah Berurah 307:16.59.*

The Jews of Shushan

Mordechai

Esther

The King's Guards

Achashverosh

Vashti

The House of Haman

Zeresh

Haman